SMITH—
WIGGLESWORTH
On the HOLY SPIRIT

SMITH— WIGGLESWORTH On the HOLY SPIRIT

Smith Wigglesworth

Whitaker House

Whitaker House gratefully acknowledges and thanks Glenn Gohr and the entire staff of the Assemblies of God Archives in Springfield, Missouri, for graciously assisting us in compiling Smith Wigglesworth's works for publication in this book.

Unless otherwise indicated, all Scripture quotations are taken from the *New King James Version* (NKJV), © 1979, 1980, 1982 by Thomas Nelson, Inc. Used by permission. All rights reserved.

Scripture quotations marked (KJV) are taken from the *King James Version* of the Bible.

SMITH WIGGLESWORTH ON THE HOLY SPIRIT

ISBN: 0-88368-544-2
Printed in the United States of America
Copyright © 1998 by Whitaker House

Whitaker House
30 Hunt Valley Circle
New Kensington, PA 15068

Library of Congress Cataloging-in-Publication Data

Wigglesworth, Smith, 1859–1947.
 Smith Wigglesworth on the Holy Spirit / by Smith Wigglesworth.
  p. cm.
 ISBN 0-88368-544-2
 1. Holy Spirit—Sermons. 2. Pentecostal churches—Sermons.
3. Sermons, English. I. Title.
BT122.W56 1998
234'.13—dc21   98-33350

1 2 3 4 5 6 7 8 9 10 11 12 / 08 07 06 05 04 03 02 01 00 99

Contents

Introduction.. 7

1. The Baptism in the Holy Spirit.......................... 13
2. Foundational Truths of the Baptism.................. 19
3. The Fullness of the Spirit................................... 39
4. Biblical Evidence of the Baptism....................... 45
5. Paul's Conversion and Baptism......................... 55
6. Receiving the Baptism.. 65
7. Our Heavenly Dwelling...................................... 83
8. Clothed with the Spirit..................................... 105
9. Filled with God.. 111
10. The Pentecostal Power..................................... 119
11. Christ in Us... 131
12. Aflame for God.. 153
13. "Glory and Virtue".. 159
14. The Might of the Spirit..................................... 165
15. The Place of Victory.. 179
16. "The Best with Improvement".......................... 185
17. Unconditional Surrender.................................. 203
18. New Wine... 207
19. Questions and Answers about the Baptism..... 213

Introduction

A n encounter with Smith Wigglesworth was an unforgettable experience. This seems to be the universal reaction of all who knew him or heard him speak. Smith Wigglesworth was a simple yet remarkable man who was used in an extraordinary way by our extraordinary God. He had a contagious and inspiring faith. Under his ministry, thousands of people came to salvation, committed themselves to a deeper faith in Christ, received the baptism in the Holy Spirit, and were miraculously healed. The power that brought these kinds of results was the presence of the Holy Spirit, who filled Smith Wigglesworth and used him in bringing the good news of the Gospel to people all over the world. Wigglesworth gave glory to God for everything that was accomplished through his ministry, and he wanted people to understand his work only in this context, because his sole desire was that people would see Jesus and not himself.

Smith Wigglesworth was born in England in 1859. Immediately after his conversion as a boy, he had a concern for the salvation of others and won people to Christ, including his mother. Even so, as a young man, he could not express himself well enough to give a testimony in church, much less preach a

7

sermon. Wigglesworth said that his mother had the same difficulty in expressing herself that he did. This family trait, coupled with the fact that he had no formal education because he began working twelve hours a day at the age of seven to help support the family, contributed to Wigglesworth's awkward speaking style. He became a plumber by trade, yet he continued to devote himself to winning many people to Christ on an individual basis.

In 1882, he married Polly Featherstone, a vivacious young woman who loved God and had a gift of preaching and evangelism. It was she who taught him to read and who became his closest confidant and strongest supporter. They both had compassion for the poor and needy in their community, and they opened a mission, at which Polly preached. Significantly, people were miraculously healed when Wigglesworth prayed for them.

In 1907, Wigglesworth's circumstances changed dramatically when, at the age of forty-eight, he was baptized in the Holy Spirit. Suddenly, he had a new power that enabled him to preach, and even his wife was amazed at the transformation. This was the beginning of what became a worldwide evangelistic and healing ministry that reached thousands. He eventually ministered in the United States, Australia, South Africa, and all over Europe. His ministry extended up to the time of his death in 1947.

Several emphases in Smith Wigglesworth's life and ministry characterize him: a genuine, deep compassion for the unsaved and sick; an unflinching belief in the Word of God; a desire that Christ should increase and he should decrease (John 3:30); a belief that he was called to exhort people to enlarge their faith and trust in God; an emphasis on the baptism in the Holy Spirit with the manifestation of the gifts of the Spirit as in the early church; and a belief in complete healing for everyone of all sickness.

Smith Wigglesworth was called "The Apostle of Faith" because absolute trust in God was a constant theme of both his life and his messages. In his meetings, he would quote passages from the Word of God and lead lively singing to help build people's faith and encourage them to act on it. He emphasized belief in the fact that God could do the impossible. He had great faith in what God could do, and God did great things through him.

Wigglesworth's unorthodox methods were often questioned. As a person, Wigglesworth was reportedly courteous, kind, and gentle. However, he became forceful when dealing with the Devil, whom he believed caused all sickness. Wigglesworth said the reason he spoke bluntly and acted forcefully with people was that he knew he needed to get their attention so they could focus on God. He also had such anger toward the Devil and sickness that he acted in a seemingly rough way. When he prayed for people to be healed, he would often hit or punch them at the place of their problem or illness. Yet, no one was hurt by this startling treatment. Instead, they were remarkably healed. When he was asked why he treated people in this manner, he said that he was not hitting the people but that he was hitting the Devil. He believed that Satan should never be treated gently or allowed to get away with anything. About twenty people were reportedly raised from the dead after he prayed for them. Wigglesworth himself was healed of appendicitis and kidney stones, after which his personality softened and he was more gentle with those who came to him for prayer for healing. His abrupt manner in ministering may be attributed to the fact that he was very serious about his calling and got down to business quickly.

Although Wigglesworth believed in complete healing, he encountered illnesses and deaths that were difficult to understand. These included the deaths of his wife and son, his daughter's lifelong deafness, and his own battles with kidney stones and sciatica.

He often seemed paradoxical: compassionate but forceful, gentle but blunt, a well-dressed gentleman whose speech was often ungrammatical or confusing. However, he loved God with everything he had, he was steadfastly committed to God and to His Word, and he didn't rest until he saw God move in the lives of those who needed Him.

In 1936, Smith Wigglesworth prophesied about what we now know as the charismatic movement. He accurately predicted that the established mainline denominations would experience revival and the gifts of the Spirit in a way that would surpass even the Pentecostal movement. Wigglesworth did not live to see the renewal, but as an evangelist and prophet with a remarkable healing ministry, he had a tremendous influence on both the Pentecostal and charismatic movements, and his example and influence on believers is felt to this day.

Without the power of God that was so obviously present in his life and ministry, we might not be reading transcripts of his sermons, for his spoken messages were often disjointed and ungrammatical. However, true gems of spiritual insight shine through

Introduction

them because of the revelation he received through the Holy Spirit. It was his life of complete devotion and belief in God and his reliance on the Holy Spirit that brought the life-changing power of God into his messages.

As you read this book, it is important to remember that Wigglesworth's works span a period of several decades, from the early 1900s to the 1940s. They were originally presented as spoken rather than written messages, and necessarily retain some of the flavor of a church service or prayer meeting. Some of the messages were Bible studies that Wigglesworth led at various conferences. At his meetings, he would often speak in tongues and give the interpretation, and these messages have been included as well. Because of Wigglesworth's unique style, the sermons and Bible studies in this book have been edited for clarity, and archaic expressions that would be unfamiliar to modern readers have been updated.

In conclusion, we hope that as you read these words of Smith Wigglesworth, you will truly sense his complete trust and unwavering faith in God and take to heart one of his favorite sayings: "Only believe!"

1

The Baptism in the Holy Spirit

ow glad I am that God has baptized me in the Holy Spirit. What a wonderful difference it has made in my life. God has not promised that as Christians we will always feel very wonderful, but He has promised that if we stand on His Word, He will make His Word real in our lives. First we exercise faith; then it becomes fact. However, there are plenty of feelings in the fact, I assure you. God fills us with His own precious joy.

Samson is recorded in the eleventh chapter of Hebrews as being a man of faith. He was a man who was chosen by God from his mother's womb, but the power of God came upon him only on certain occasions. Yet we who have received the fullness of the Holy Spirit, the Comforter, may now have the anointing that abides forever.

The Lord has promised that we will have life and have it abundantly (John 10:10). Look at the fifth chapter of Romans and see how many times the expression *"much more"* is used. (See, for example, Romans 5:9.) Oh, that we might take this abundant grace of God, revel in the Word of God, and be so full of expectancy that we will have this *"much more"* manifested as fruit in our lives.

THE FULLNESS OF THE SPIRIT

Some people realize that they have had the power of the Lord upon them and yet have failed to receive the fullness of the Spirit. Friend, what about you? God, in His love and kindness, has listed Samson in Hebrews 11 as an example for us. There came a time when, because of Samson's sin, his eyes were put out. His hair had been cut off, and he had lost his strength. He tried to break free of his bonds, but the Philistines got him. However, his hair grew again. The Philistines wanted him to entertain for them, but he prayed a prayer, and God answered. Oh, that we might turn to God and pray this prayer, as Samson did: *"O Lord GOD, remember me, I pray! Strengthen me, I pray, just this once, O God"* (Judg. 16:28). God is *"plenteous in mercy"* (Ps. 86:5 KJV), and if you will turn to Him with true repentance, He will forgive you. Repentance means getting back to God.

When Samson took hold of the pillars upon which the Philistine house stood, he pulled the walls down (Judg. 16:29–30). God can give you strength, and you can get hold of the posts, and He will work through you. No matter what kind of a backslider you have been, there is power in the blood. *"The blood of Jesus Christ His Son cleanses us from all sin"* (1 John 1:7). Oh, if I could only tell you how

The Baptism in the Holy Spirit

God so wonderfully restored me! I returned to my *"first love"* (Rev. 2:4), and He filled me with the Holy Spirit.

I want to draw your attention to a few verses from the second chapter of the Acts of the Apostles:

> *When the Day of Pentecost had fully come, they were all with one accord in one place. And suddenly there came a sound from heaven, as of a rushing mighty wind, and it filled the whole house where they were sitting. Then there appeared to them divided tongues, as of fire, and one sat upon each of them. And they were all filled with the Holy Spirit and began to speak with other tongues, as the Spirit gave them utterance.* (Acts 2:1–4)

What a wonderful, divine position God intends us all to have, to be filled with the Holy Spirit. It is something so remarkable, so divine; it is, as it were, a great open door into all the treasury of the Most High. As the Spirit comes like *"rain upon the mown grass"* (Ps. 72:6 KJV), He turns the barrenness into greenness and freshness and life. Oh, hallelujah! God wants you to know that there is a place you may come to, in which you are dispensed with and God comes to be your assurance and sustaining power spiritually—until your dryness is turned into springs, until your barrenness becomes floods, until your whole life becomes vitalized by heaven, until heaven sweeps through you and dwells within you and turns everything inside out, until you are so absolutely filled with divine possibilities that you begin to live as a new creation. The Spirit of the living God sweeps through all weaknesses.

Beloved, God the Holy Spirit wants to bring us to a great revelation of life. He wants us to be filled with all the fullness of God. One of the most beautiful pictures we have in the Scriptures is of the Trinity. The Trinity was made manifest right on the banks of the Jordan River when Jesus was baptized. I want you to see how God unfolded heaven and how heaven and earth became the habitation of the Trinity. The voice of God came from the heavens as He looked at His well-beloved Son coming out of the waters, and there the Spirit was manifested in the shape of a dove. The dove is the only bird without gall; it is a creature so timid that at the least thing it moves and is afraid. No person can be baptized with the Holy Spirit and have bitterness, that is, gall.

A DOUBLE CURE

My friend, you need a double cure. You first need saving and cleansing and then the baptism of the Holy Spirit, until the old man never rises anymore, until you are absolutely dead to sin and alive to God by His Spirit and know that old things have passed away. When the Holy Spirit gets possession of a person, he is a new man entirely—his whole being becomes saturated with divine power. We become a habitation of Him who is all light, all revelation, all power, and all love. Yes, God the Holy Spirit is manifested within us in such a way that it is glorious.

There was a certain rich man in London whose business flourished. He used to count all his many assets, but he was still troubled inside; he didn't know what to do. Walking around his large building, he came upon a boy who was the doorkeeper and found the boy whistling. Looking at him, he sized up the whole situation completely and went back to his office again and puzzled over the matter. He went back to his business but he could find no peace. His bank could not help him; his money, his success, could not help him. He had an aching void. He was helpless within. My friend, having the world without having God is like being a whitewashed sepulcher. (See Matthew 23:27.)

When he could get no rest, he exclaimed, "I will go and see what the boy is doing." Again he went and found him whistling. "I want you to come into my office," he said. When they entered the office, the man said, "Tell me, what makes you so happy and cheerful?" "Oh," replied the boy, "I used to be so miserable until I went to a little mission and heard about Jesus. Then I was saved and filled with the Holy Spirit. I am always whistling inside; if I am not whistling, I am singing. I am just full!"

This rich man obtained the address of the mission from the boy, went to the services, and sat beside the door. But the power of God moved so strongly that when the altar call was given, he responded. God saved him and, a few days afterward, filled him with the Holy Spirit. The man found himself at his desk, shouting, "Oh, hallelujah!"

> I know the Lord, I know the Lord,
> I know the Lord's laid His hand on me.
> I know the Lord, I know the Lord,
> I know the Lord's laid His hand on me.

Oh, this blessed Son of God wants to fill us with such glory until our whole body is aflame with the power of the Holy Spirit. I see there is *"much more"* (Rom. 5:9). Glory to God! My daughter asked some African boys to tell us the difference between being saved and being filled with the Holy Spirit. "Ah," they said, "when we were saved, it was very good; but when we received the Holy Spirit, it was more so." Many of you have never received the "more so."

After the Holy Spirit comes upon you, you will have power. God will mightily move within your life; the power of the Holy Spirit will overshadow you, inwardly moving you until you know there is a divine plan different from anything that you have had in your life before.

Has He come? He is going to come to you. I am expecting that God will so manifest His presence and power that He will show you the necessity of receiving the Holy Spirit. Also, God will heal the people who need healing. Everything is to be had now: salvation, sanctification, the fullness of the Holy Spirit, and healing. God is working mightily by the power of His Spirit, bringing to us a fullness of His perfect redemption until every soul may know that God has all power.

2

Foundational Truths of the Baptism

hat it means for people to have faith! What it will mean when we all have faith! We know that as soon as faith is in perfect operation, we will be in the perfect place where God is manifested right before our eyes. The pure in heart will see God (Matt. 5:8), and all the steps of purity are a divine appointment of more faith. The more purity, the more faith.

When Lazarus died and Jesus knew that Mary, Martha, and everyone around them had lost confidence and faith, He turned to the Father in prayer and said, *"Father...I know that You always hear Me"* (John 11:41–42). Jesus commanded Lazarus to come out of the tomb; death had to give him up, and everything had to come to pass as He said.

Fellowship, purity, unity: these things reflect a living cooperation in which we are being changed from faith to faith. May the Lord grant to you this thought today: How may I more and more abandon myself from any earthly, human fellowship, until I am absolutely so bound to God that God has the right-of-way to the throne of my heart, until the seat of affection is blessedly purified, until there is no room for anything except the Son of God, who is the Author and Finisher of faith (Heb. 12:2)? Then Christ will be manifested in your flesh, destroying everything that is outside of Him.

When the Spirit of the Lord is upon us, we do not impart words but life. Words are only for the purpose of understanding what the Word is, but the Word itself is really life-giving. So when we are covered with the Spirit, we are imparting life. When we are filled with the Holy Spirit, every time we get up, we impart life. If you are ready to receive this life, it is amazing how it will quicken your mortal body every time you touch this life. (See Romans 8:11.) It is divine life. It is the life of the Son of God.

I want to lay down a foundation for understanding the baptism of the Holy Spirit by explaining why Jesus emphasized the baptism, how to receive the baptism, and the reason for the baptism. Jesus expressed all these things to His disciples. I want to dwell on this in order to provide you with a real foundation of the truth of the baptism. In this way, you will never wait before God without a clear understanding of what the baptism is for, what you are waiting for, and so on.

To begin with, we find a remarkable word from John the Baptist in Matthew 3:11:

> *I indeed baptize you with water unto repentance, but He who is coming after me is mightier than I, whose sandals I am not worthy to*

*carry. He will baptize you with the Holy Spirit
and fire.*

This is the statement of a man who was so filled
with the Spirit of God that his very voice became the
active process of a divine flame that moved the
whole of creation that day. From east to west and
north to south, he spoke by the power of the Holy
Spirit until people gathered at the Jordan in multitudes, drawn by this voice of one crying in the Spirit.
(See Matthew 3:3.) What a remarkable word he
gave!

IMMERSED WITH THE SPIRIT

Most of us have seen water baptism in action so
often that we know what it means. But I want you to
see that God's very great desire is for you to be covered with the baptism of the Holy Spirit. He wants
you to be so immersed and covered and flooded with
the light and revelation of the Holy Spirit, the third
person of the Trinity, that your whole body will be
filled, and not only filled but also covered over until
you walk in the presence of the power of God.

Interpretation of Tongues

God's life for your life, His light for your
darkness, His revelation for your closed brain.
He brings forth a new order in divine power
until you will be changed into another man,
until your very nature will be burning with a
burning within you of divine purifying until
you are like one who has come from the presence of the Glory to exhibit truths that God

21

has revealed to you. In your lot, in your day, the power of another covering, girding you with the power of truth.

Oh, Jesus, let it come to pass that we never do anything in our own strength. Let all that we do be done to the glory of the Lord!

COME TO THE WATERS

We cannot stop there; that was the first breath of revelation of what would take place for individuals—yes, and for communities and for the world.

Let us turn now to John 7:37–39:

On the last day, that great day of the feast, Jesus stood and cried out, saying, "If anyone thirsts, let him come to Me and drink. He who believes in Me, as the Scripture has said, out of his heart will flow rivers of living water." But this He spoke concerning the Spirit, whom those believing in Him would receive; for the Holy Spirit was not yet given, because Jesus was not yet glorified.

Jesus saw all the people at the Feast of Tabernacles, and He not only had a great ability to scrutinize, to unfold the inward thoughts and intents of the heart, but He also saw things at a glance; He took in a situation in just a moment's time. He knew when the people were about to starve and die by the wayside, and He supplied all their needs.

We must not forget that He was filled with the Holy Spirit. He was lovely because He was full of the divine inflow of the life of God. Look at how He dealt with this situation. He saw the people who had been at Jerusalem at the feast, and they were coming back dissatisfied. My Lord could not have anybody dissatisfied. My Lord could never be satisfied when anybody was dissatisfied.

It is not in the canon of the history of the spiritual fellowship between heaven and earth that you should be famished, naked, full of discord, full of evil, full of disorder, full of sensuality, full of carnality. That was what was taking place at the feast, and they came away hungrier than they were before. Jesus saw them like that, and He said, "*'Ho! Everyone who thirsts, come to the waters'* (Isa. 55:1). Come to Me, you who are thirsty, and I will give you drink."

Oh, the Master could give! The Master had it to give. Beloved, He is here to give, and I am sure He will give.

Interpretation of Tongues

God, First, Last, Alpha, Omega, Beginning and End. He is at the root of all things this morning. He will disturb what needs to be disturbed; He will unfold what needs to be unfolded; He will turn to death what needs to be broken and put to death. He will put a spring within you and lift you to life. God will deal with you in mercy but in severity, because all divine love is a sword and "divides asunder soul and spirit, joint and marrow," and deals with the inward desires of the heart.

Yes, the heavy hand of God is full of mercy. The two-edged sword is full of dividing. His quickening Spirit puts to death everything that needs to die so that He might transform you by the resurrection of His life.

And this is the order of the Spirit. Can't you see how He says, "Come, thirsty one; come, needy one. I will give you a drink that will create a thirst in you that will prepare you for the coming of the Holy Spirit, that will make the spring that I give you a river of living water"?

Which do you have? Do you have the spring or the river? The spring is good because it has the same kind of water as the river. But the river means plentifulness, and the Holy Spirit is the river. Jesus was portraying, forecasting, sending out these wonderful words so that He might prepare the people for all the fullness that had to come forth.

BE EXTRAORDINARY

I want you to go away from these meetings just infused. Make up your mind that you won't be ordinary. You have an extraordinary God who gives revelation. Be determined that you won't go away as you came but that you will go away endued, infused with the living touch of the flame of the Master's torch.

These are not ordinary meetings; God would not want a meeting to be ordinary. I refuse to be an ordinary man. "Why?" you ask. Because I have an extraordinary God who makes extraordinary people, and because we either believe God's plan or we do not.

When we speak this way, we are at the root of the matter that can bring forth anything. Because Abram believed God, every person is blessed today through faithful Abraham. (See Galatians 3:8–9.) He was an extraordinary man of faith; he believed God in the face of everything.

You would like to be extraordinary, wouldn't you? If you are prayed for this morning, though you see no change at all, if you believe it is done, you may become extraordinary in that way. You who have been longing for the baptism of the Holy Spirit and have been waiting and tarrying every day, if you have come to a place of believing, you have come to a place where you have become extraordinary.

Interpretation of Tongues

The peace that comes from above is always full of purity and life-giving, and it never brings destruction to anyone. And the wisdom is on the same line; and all purification on every line never disturbs you. It is only what is earthly that disturbs you. You cannot be disturbed by a heavenly breath. God is with us on a heavenly breath, and in that action you cannot be disturbed. If you are disturbed from this day, know it is an earthly thing that is disturbing you.

GREATER WORKS

Now I want to explain the fourteenth chapter of John. It is the Master's word; it is the Master's desire. He said to His disciples in the twelfth verse, *"Greater works than these* [you] *will do."* Why was His perspective so full? Because He had admiration before Him. Jesus had great admiration before Him when He saw the disciples. He knew He had the material that would bring out what would prove to be a real satisfaction to the world—to heaven and to the world. The glorified, trained, wonderfully modified, and then again glorified positions of these fishermen were surely ideal places in which to be.

What were the disciples? For one thing, they were unlearned (not that I am going to build on an unlearned position). For another thing, they were ignorant men (not that I am going to build on ignorance, either). However, note this: they were unlearned, but God taught them. It is far better to have the learning of the Spirit than anything else. They were ignorant; He enlarged them. They were beside themselves because they had been touched with the divine life. If the Most High God touches you, you will be beside yourself. As long as you hold your own, the natural and the spiritual will be mixed; but if you ever jump over the lines by the power of the new creation, you will find He has gotten a hold of you.

Divine wisdom will never make you foolish. Divine wisdom will give you a sound mind; divine wisdom will give you a touch of divine nature. Divine life is full of divine appointment and equipping, and you cannot be filled with the power of God without a manifestation. It is my prayer today that we would understand that to be filled with the Holy Spirit is to be filled with manifestation, the glory of the Lord being in the midst of us, manifesting His divine power.

Jesus knew that these people He had before Him were going to do greater things than He had done (John 14:12). How could they do them? None of us is able; none of us is capable. But our incapability has to be clothed with His divine ability, and our helplessness has to be filled with His power of helpfulness. This is why He knew that they would do greater things.

He knew that He was going away and that, if He went away, it was expedient, it was necessary, it was important that Another come in His place and take up the same thing in them as He had been telling them (John 16:7, 14 KJV). *"You in Me, and I in you"* (John 14:20). There was a plan of divine order. So the Holy Spirit was to come.

I want you to see what has to take place when the Holy Spirit comes:

> *And I will pray the Father, and he shall give you another Comforter, that he may abide with you for ever; even the Spirit of truth; whom the world cannot receive, because it seeth him not, neither knoweth him: but ye know him; for he dwelleth with you, and shall be in you. I will not leave you comfortless: I will come to you.*
> *(vv. 16–18 KJV)*

I don't know a word that could be as fitting at this time as this word *"Comforter."* I want to take you with me into the coming of this Holy Spirit.

After Jesus ascended to heaven, He asked the Father to send the Comforter. It was a needy moment, a needy hour, a necessity. Why? Because the disciples would need comforting.

How could they be comforted? The Holy Spirit would take the word of Christ and reveal it to them (John 16:14). What could help them as much as a word by the Spirit? For the Spirit is breath, is life, is person, is power. He gives the breath of Himself to us, the nature of Him. How beautiful that, when the Spirit came, He should be called the *"Spirit of truth."* Oh, if we would only read that into our hearts!

Some people have wondered that if they were to ask for the baptism of the Holy Spirit, if an evil power could come instead or if an evil power could possess them while they were waiting for the Holy Spirit. Why, when you receive the Holy Spirit, you receive the Spirit of Truth, the Spirit who gives revelation, the Spirit who takes the words of Jesus and makes them life to you. In your moment of need, He is the Comforter.

What will the Holy Spirit do? The Holy Spirit is prophetic. He says: *"Be of good cheer"* (John 16:33). *"Take My yoke upon you and learn from Me"* (Matt. 11:29). *"Have peace with one another"* (Mark 9:50). You say, "But that is what Jesus said." It is what the Holy Spirit is taking and revealing to us and speaking to us. The Holy Spirit is the spokesman in these days. The Holy Spirit came to be the spokesman, and He spoke the Word. He is still taking the Word and speaking it. The Holy Spirit takes the words of Jesus, and He is so full of truth that He never adds anything to them. He gives you the unadulterated Word of Truth, the Word of Life.

"He will take of Mine and declare [reveal] *it to you"* (John 16:15). What is His? Truths like these: *"I am the light of the world"* (8:12), and *"For God did not send His Son into the world to condemn the world, but that the world through Him might be saved"* (3:17). The Holy Spirit takes these words and gives them to you. Here are some of the words of the

Master: *"Come to Me, all you who labor and are heavy laden, and I will give you rest"* (Matt. 11:28).

Who is speaking? It is the Holy Spirit in the last days, the Spirit of Truth bringing forth the Word of Life. *"I will give you rest."* Rest? Oh, there is no rest like it! It can come in your moment of greatest trial.

When my dear wife was lying dead, the doctors could do nothing, and they said to me, "She is done; we cannot help you." My heart was so moved, and I said, "O God, I can't spare her!"

I went up to her and I said, "Oh, come back, come back and speak to me. Come back, come back!"

And the Spirit of the Lord moved, and she came back and smiled again.

Then the Holy Spirit said to me, "She is mine. Her work is done; she is mine."

Oh, the comforting word! No one else could have done it, but the Comforter came. At that moment, my dear wife passed away.

Ah, beloved, it is true to me that the Comforter has a word for us this day. He is the Comforter. There is only one Comforter, and He has been with the Father from the beginning. He comes only to give light. When the Holy Spirit comes into your body, He comes to unveil the King, to assure you of His presence.

BE SPECIFIC IN WHAT YOU ASK

The person who says "I am ready for anything" will never get it.

"What are you seeking, my brother?"

"Oh, I am ready for anything."

"You will never get 'anything.'"

"Oh! Well, tell me how to get it, then."

"One thing I have desired of the LORD, that will I seek" (Ps. 27:4). When the Lord reveals to you that you must be filled with the Holy Spirit, seek only that one thing, and God will give you that one thing. It is necessary for you to seek one thing first.

In a meeting one day, I went to two young men and said to them, "Young men, what about it? Would you like to receive the baptism?" They had just earned their degrees, and they were handsome young men.

"Oh!" they said. "We don't believe in it the same way you do. We don't believe in receiving the Holy Spirit as those people do."

There was a crowd of people waiting in the front.

"You are dressed up as if you would like to have it," I said. "You are dressed like preachers, and seeing that you are dressed like preachers, it is a pity for you to have the clothing without the Presence."

"Well, we don't believe it that way," they said.

"But look," I said, "the apostles believed it that way. Wouldn't you like to be an apostle? Wouldn't you like to go along the same lines as they did? They believed it that way."

Never forget, the baptism will always be as it was in the beginning. It has not changed. And if you want a real baptism, expect it to be just the same as they had it at the beginning.

"What did they have at the beginning?" you ask.

Well, the early believers knew when others had the same experience they had had at the beginning, for they heard them speak in tongues. That is the only way they did know, because they heard the others saying the same things in the Spirit that they had said at the beginning. It has never been changed; it has always been the same right down to today. As it was in the beginning, so it will be forever and ever.

When these two young men at the meeting realized that Peter and John and the rest of them had the baptism, they came up to receive it. They were beautifully dressed. In about half an hour's time, they looked strange. They had been rolling, somehow. I had not caused them to do it. But they had been so lost in and so controlled by the power of God that they were just rolling all around and their clothes were rumpled—but their faces were wonderful.

What had happened? They had received it just as the first Christians had received it at the beginning.

These young men had been ordained as pastors by men. I do not say anything against that; I think that is very good. However, there is an ordination that is better, and it is the ordination with the King. This is the only ordination that is going to equip you for the future. The King is already on His throne, but He needs crowning; when the Holy Spirit comes, He crowns the King inside of us.

The person who has passed through that ordination goes forth with fresh feet—the preparation of the Gospel (Eph. 6:15); he goes forth with a fresh voice, speaking as the Spirit gives utterance (Acts 2:4); he goes forth with a fresh mind, his mind being illuminated by the power of God (see Hebrews 8:10); he goes forth with a fresh vision and sees all things new. (See 2 Corinthians 5:17.)

When the Holy Spirit comes, He will reveal things to you. Has He revealed them yet? He is going to do it. Just expect Him to do so. The best thing for you is to expect Him to do it now.

OVERCOMING HINDRANCES TO RECEIVING

Put up with any disorder you like when you are coming through into the baptism. As far as I am concerned, you can have the biggest time on earth; you can scream as much as you like. Yet some people are frightened by this.

A woman in Switzerland came to me after I had helped her and asked to speak to me further.

"Now that I feel I am healed," she said, "and that terrible carnal passion that has bound and hindered me is gone, I feel that I have a new mind. I believe I would like to receive the Holy Spirit, but when I hear these people screaming, I feel like running away."

After that, we were at another meeting in Switzerland where a large hotel was joined to the building. At the close of one of the morning services, the power of God fell—that is the only way I can describe it, the power of God *fell*. This poor, timid creature who couldn't bear to hear anybody scream, screamed so loud that all the waiters in this big hotel came out with their aprons on and with their trays to see what was up. Nothing was especially up. Something had come down, and it had so altered the situation that this woman could stand anything after that.

When God begins dealing with you on the baptism, He begins on this line: He starts with the things that are the most difficult. He starts with your fear; He starts with your human nature. He puts the fear away; He gets the human nature out of the way. And just as you dissolve, just as the power of the Spirit brings a dissolving to your human nature, in the same act the Holy Spirit flows into the place where you are being dissolved, and you are quickened just where you come into death. As you die, naturally, humanly, carnally, selfishly, to every evil thing, the new life, the Holy Spirit, floods the whole condition until it becomes a transformed condition.

"No man can tame the tongue" (James 3:8); but when the Holy Spirit begins, He tames the whole body until the tongue, moved by the power of the Spirit, says things exactly as the Lord would be delighted for them to be said.

The Holy Spirit is the Comforter; the Holy Spirit takes the necessary word at the right time and gives it to you. After the Holy Spirit takes charge of you, He is the Comforter who brings thought and language to your life, and it is amazing.

If we get to the place where we take no thought for ourselves, then God takes thought for us; but as long as we are taking thought for ourselves, we are somewhat hindered in this divine order with God. Taking no thought for yourself, no desire for your human self, not seeking anything for your human condition but that God will be glorified in your body and spirit and that He will be the chief Worker on every line—this is divine appointment. This is holy order.

There is a holy order. There are sects today that call themselves "holy orders," but the only holy order is where God has gotten so through with your nature that the Trinity comes and blends perfectly with your human nature. Where the human nature could not help itself, God turned the captivity of the wheels of nature and poured in His divine power until the nature itself became divine property.

YOU HAVE AN ANOINTING

Another of the roles of the Holy Spirit that is necessary for today we find in John 14:26:

> *But the Comforter, which is the Holy* [Spirit], *whom the Father will send in my name, he shall teach you all things, and bring all things to your remembrance, whatsoever I have said unto you.* (KJV)

Jesus said something very similar in a later chapter: *"He will take of what is Mine and declare* [reveal] *it to you"* (John 16:14). Everything that has been revealed to you was first taken. So, first, the Holy Spirit takes of what is Christ's and reveals it to you. Then you come to the place where you need another touch. What is it? In the necessity of your ministry, He will bring to your remembrance everything that you need in your ministry. That is an important thing for preachers. God will give us His Word, and if there is anything special we need, He will bring that to our memories, too. The Holy Spirit comes to bring the Word to us in remembrance.

I will throw this word out to you as a help for future reflection. In 1 John 2:20, we read, *"You have an anointing from the Holy One."* May God grant that we will not forget it! *"You shall receive power"* (Acts 1:8). Oh, may God grant that we will not forget it!

What do I mean by that? Many people, instead of standing on the rock-solid word of faith and believing that they have received the baptism with its anointing and power, say, "Oh, if I could only feel that I have received it!"

My friend, your feelings rob you of your greatest place of anointing. Your feelings are a place very often of discouragement. You have to get away from the sense of all human feeling or desire. Earthly desires are not God's desires. All thoughts of holiness, all thoughts of purity, all thoughts of power from the Holy Spirit are from above. Human thoughts are like clouds that belong to the earth. "[God's] *thoughts are not* [our] *thoughts*" (Isa. 55:8).

Interpretation of Tongues

It is the shadows that flee away. It is your feelings that have to be moved from you this day. It is the divine unction of a new creation moving in your human nature that has to change all, even your environment, and make you so that your heart, even your mind and your tongue and everything, will be in a place of magnifying the Lord. Remember, it is from above in your heart to change all your life until you will be as He has promised, sons of God with power.

"You have an anointing" (1 John 2:20).

Some things are of necessity. Suppose that all around me are people with needs: a woman is dying; a man has lost all the powers of his faculties; another person is apparently dying. Here they are. I see the great need, and I drop down on my knees and cry. Yet in doing so, I miss it all.

God does not want me to cry. God does not want me to labor. God does not want me to anguish and to be filled with anxiety and a sorrowful spirit. What does He want me to do?

Only believe. After you have received, only believe. Come to the authority of it; dare to believe. Say, "I will do it!"

So the baptism of the Holy Spirit says to me, *"You have an anointing."* The anointing has come; the anointing remains; the anointing is with us. But what if you have not lived in the place in which the unction, the anointing, can be increased? Ah! Then the Spirit is grieved; then you are not moved. You are like one who is dead. You feel that all the joy is gone.

What is the matter? There is something between you and the Holy One; you are not clean, not pure, not desirous of Him alone. Something else has come in the way. Then the Spirit is grieved, and you have lost the unction.

Is the Unctioner still there? Yes. When He comes in, He comes to remain. He will either be grieved, full of groaning and travail, or He will be there to lift you above the powers of darkness, transform you by His power, and take you to a place where you may be fully equipped.

Many people lose all potential positions of attainment because they fail to understand this:

> *But the anointing which you have received from Him abides in you, and you do not need that anyone teach you; but as the same anointing teaches you concerning all things, and is true, and is not a lie, and just as it has taught you, you will abide in Him.* *(1 John 2:27)*

What *"anointing"* is referred to here? *"God anointed Jesus of Nazareth with the Holy Spirit and with power, who went about doing good"* (Acts 10:38). The same anointing is with you, *"and you do not need that anyone teach you."* The same anointing is with you and will teach you all things.

O lovely Jesus! Blessed Incarnation of holy display! Thank God for the Trinity displayed in our hearts today. Thank God for this glorious open way. Thank God for darkness that is turning into day. Thank God for life all along the way. Praise God for hope that we may all be changed today. Hallelujah!

> Peace, peace, sweet peace,
> Coming down from the Father above,
> Peace, peace, wonderful peace,
> Sweet peace, the gift of God's love.

This is the very position and presence that will bring everybody into a fullness.

3

The Fullness
of the Spirit

*And now abide faith, hope, love, these three; but the
greatest of these is love. Pursue love, and desire
spiritual gifts, but especially that you may prophesy.
For he who speaks in a tongue does not speak to men
but to God, for no one understands him; however, in
the spirit he speaks mysteries. But he who prophesies
speaks edification and exhortation
and comfort to men.*
—1 Corinthians 13:13–14:3

t is quite easy to construct a building if the
foundation is secure. On the other hand, a
building will be unstable if it does not have
a solid understructure. Likewise, it is not
very easy to rise spiritually unless we have a real
spiritual power working within us. It will never do
for us to be top-heavy—the base must always be very
firmly set. Many of us have not gone on in the Lord
because we have not had a secure foundation in
Him, and we will have to consider *"the pit from
which [we] were dug"* (Isa. 51:1). Unless we correctly

39

understand the spiritual leadings, according to the mind of God, we will never be able to stand when the winds blow, when the trials come, and when Satan appears as *"an angel of light"* (2 Cor. 11:14). We will never be able to stand unless we are firmly fixed in the Word of God.

There must be three things in our lives if we wish to go all the way with God in the fullness of Pentecost. First, we must be grounded and settled in love; we must have a real knowledge of what love is. Secondly, we must have a clear understanding of the Word, for love must manifest the Word. Thirdly, we must clearly understand our own ground, because it is our own ground that needs to be looked after the most.

The Lord speaks at least twice of the good ground into which seed was sown, which also bore fruit and brought forth some one hundredfold, and some sixty, and some thirty (Matt. 13:8; Mark 4:8). Even in the good ground, the seed yielded different portions of fruit. I maintain truly that there is no limitation to the abundance of a harvest when the ground is perfectly in the hands of the Lord. So we must clearly understand that the Word of God can never come forth with all its primary purposes unless our ground is right. But God will help us, I believe, to see that He can make the ground in perfect order as it is put into His hands.

Let me speak about 1 Corinthians 13:13, and then I must continue on quickly. I want you to notice that the primary thought in the mind of the Spirit is that when love is in perfect progress, all other things will work in harmony, for prophetic utterances are all of no value unless they are perfectly covered with divine love. Our Lord Jesus would never have accomplished His great plan in this world except that He was so full of love for His Father, and love for us, that love never failed to accomplish its purpose. It worked in Him and through Him by the power of the Father's love in Him.

I believe that love will have to come into our lives. Christ must be the summit, the desire, the plan of all things. All our sayings, doings, and workings must be well pleasing in and to Him, and then our prophetic utterances will be a blessing through God; they will never be side issues. There is no imitation in a man filled with the Holy Spirit. Imitation is lost as the great plan of Christ becomes the ideal of his life.

God wants you to be so balanced in spiritual anointing that you will always be able to do what pleases Him, and not what will please other people or yourself. The ideal must be that it will all be to edification, and everything must go on to this end to please the Lord.

"Pursue love, and desire spiritual gifts, but especially that you may prophesy" (1 Cor. 14:1). When someone came to Moses and said that there were two others in the camp prophesying, Moses said, *"Oh, that all the Lord's people were prophets"* (Num. 11:29). That is a clear revelation along these lines that God wants us to be in such a spiritual, holy place that He could take our words and so fill them with divine power that we would speak only as the Spirit leads in prophetic utterances.

Beloved, there is spiritual language, and there is also human language, which always stays on the human plane. The divine comes into the same language so that it is changed by spiritual power and brings life to those who hear you speak. But this divine touch of prophecy will never come in any way except through the infilling of the Spirit.

If you wish to be anything for God, do not miss His plan. God has no room for you on ordinary lines. You must realize that within you there is the power of the Holy Spirit, who is forming within you everything you require.

I believe we have too much preaching and too little testifying. You will never have a living Pentecostal church with a preacher who is every night preaching, preaching, preaching. The people get tired of this constant preaching, but they never get tired when the whole place is on fire, when twenty or more jump up at once and will not sit down until they testify. So, remember, you must awake out of your lethargy.

> *And it shall come to pass afterward that I will pour out My Spirit on all flesh; your sons and your daughters shall prophesy, your old men shall dream dreams, your young men shall see visions. And also on My menservants and on My maidservants I will pour out My Spirit in those days.* *(Joel 2:28–29)*

This was spoken by the prophet Joel, and we know that this is what occurred on the Day of Pentecost. This was the first outpouring of the Spirit, but what would it be like now if we would only wake up to the words of our Master, *"Greater works than these* [you] *will do, because I go to My Father"* (John 14:12)?

The Fullness of the Spirit

Hear what the Scripture says to us: *"However, when He, the Spirit of truth, has come, He will guide you into all truth; for He will not speak on His own authority, but whatever He hears He will speak"* (John 16:13). The Holy Spirit is inspiration; the Holy Spirit is revelation; the Holy Spirit is manifestation; the Holy Spirit is operation. When a man comes into the fullness of the Holy Spirit, he is in perfect order, built up on scriptural foundations.

I have failed to see any man understand the twelfth, thirteenth, and fourteenth chapters of 1 Corinthians unless he had been baptized with the Holy Spirit. He may talk about the Holy Spirit and the gifts, but his understanding is only a superficial one. However, when he gets baptized with the Holy Spirit, he speaks about a deep inward conviction by the power of the Spirit working in him, a revelation of that Scripture. On the other hand, there is so much that a man receives when he is born again. He receives the first love and has a revelation of Jesus. *"But if we walk in the light as He is in the light, we have fellowship with one another, and the blood of Jesus Christ His Son cleanses us from all sin"* (1 John 1:7).

But God wants a man to be on fire so that he will always speak as an oracle of God. He wants to so build that man on the foundations of God that everyone who sees and hears him will say he is a new man after the order of the Spirit. *"Old things have passed away; behold, all things have become new"* (2 Cor. 5:17). New things have come, and he is now in the divine order. When a man is filled with the Holy Spirit, he has a vital power that makes people know he has seen God. He ought to be in such a place spiritually that when he goes into a neighbor's house, or out among people, they will feel that God has come into their midst.

"He who prophesies speaks edification and exhortation and comfort to men. He who speaks in a tongue edifies himself, but he who prophesies edifies the church" (1 Cor. 14:3–4). There are two edifications spoken of here. Which is the first? To edify yourself. After you have been edified by the Spirit, you are able to edify the church through the Spirit. What we need is more of the Holy Spirit. Oh, beloved, it is not merely a measure of the Spirit, it is a pressed-down measure. It is not merely a pressed-down measure, it is *"shaken together, and running over"* (Luke 6:38). Anybody can hold a full cup, but you cannot hold an overflowing cup, and the baptism of the Holy Spirit is an overflowing cup. Praise the Lord!

4

Biblical Evidence of the Baptism

here is much controversy today regarding the genuineness of this Pentecostal work. However, there is nothing so convincing as the fact that over twenty-five years ago, a revival on Holy Spirit lines began and has never ceased. You will find that in every region throughout the world, God has poured out His Spirit in a remarkable way, in a manner parallel to the glorious revival that inaugurated the church of the first century.

Our Lord Jesus said to His disciples, *"Behold, I send the Promise of My Father upon you; but tarry in the city of Jerusalem until you are endued with power from on high"* (Luke 24:49). God promised through the prophet Joel, *"I will pour out My Spirit on all flesh....On My menservants and on My maidservants I will pour out My Spirit in those days"* (Joel 2:28–29).

TONGUES AND THE BAPTISM

Let me tell you about my own experience of being baptized with the Holy Spirit. You know, beloved, that it had to be something that was based on solid facts in order to move me. I was as certain as possible that I had received the Holy Spirit, and I was absolutely rigid in this conviction. Many years ago, a man came to me and said, "Wigglesworth, do you know what is happening in Sunderland, England? People are being baptized in the Holy Spirit exactly the same way that the disciples were on the Day of Pentecost." I said, "I would like to go."

Immediately, I took a train and went to Sunderland and met with the people who had assembled for the purpose of receiving the Holy Spirit. I was continuously in those meetings causing disturbances, until the people wished I had never come. They said that I was disrupting the conditions for people to receive the baptism. But I was hungry and thirsty for God, and had gone to Sunderland because I had heard that God was pouring out His Spirit in a new way. I had heard that God had now visited His people and manifested His power, and that people were speaking in tongues as on the Day of Pentecost.

Therefore, when I first got to Sunderland, I said to the people, "I cannot understand this meeting. I have left a meeting in Bradford all on fire for God. The fire fell last night, and we were all laid out under the power of God. I have come here for tongues, and I don't hear them—I don't hear anything."

"Oh!" they said. "When you get baptized with the Holy Spirit, you will speak in tongues."

"Oh, is that it?" I said. "When the presence of God came upon me, my tongue was loosened, and when I went in the open air to preach, I really felt that I had a new tongue."

"Ah, no," they said, "that is not it."

"What is it, then?" I asked.

"When you get baptized in the Holy Spirit—"

"I am baptized," I interjected, "and there is no one here who can persuade me that I am not baptized."

So I was up against them, and they were up against me.

I remember a man getting up and saying, "You know, brothers and sisters, I was here three weeks and then the Lord baptized me with the Holy Spirit, and I began to speak with tongues."

I said, "Let us hear it. That's what I'm here for."

But he could not speak in tongues at will; he could only speak as the Spirit gave him the ability, and so my curiosity was not satisfied. I was doing what others are doing today, confusing the twelfth chapter of 1 Corinthians with the second chapter of Acts. These two chapters deal with different things; one deals with the gifts of the Spirit, and the other deals with the baptism of the Spirit with the accompanying sign of tongues.

I saw that these people were very earnest, and I became quite hungry for tongues. I was eager to see this new manifestation of the Spirit, and, as I said, I would be questioning all the time and spoiling a lot of the meetings. One man said to me, "I am a missionary, and I have come here to seek the baptism in the Holy Spirit. I am waiting on the Lord, but you have come in and are spoiling everything with your questions." I began to argue with him; the argument became so heated that when we walked home, he walked on one side of the road, and I walked on the other.

That night, there was to be another meeting, and I purposed to go. I changed my clothes and left my key in the clothes I had taken off. As we came from the meeting in the middle of the night, I found that I did not have my key with me, and this missionary brother said, "You will have to come and stay with me." But do you think we went to sleep that night? Oh, no, we spent the night in prayer. We received a precious shower from above. The breakfast bell rang, but that was nothing to me. For four days, I wanted nothing but God. If you only knew the unspeakably wonderful blessing of being filled with the third person of the Trinity, you would set aside everything else to wait for this infilling.

As the days passed, I became more and more hungry for God. I had opposed the meetings so much, but the Lord was gracious, and I will always remember that last day—the day I was to leave. God was with me so much. They were to have a meeting, and I went, but I could not rest. This revival was taking place at an Episcopal church. I went to the rectory to say goodbye, and I said to Sister Boddy, the rector's wife, "I cannot rest any longer; I must have these tongues."

She replied, "Brother Wigglesworth, it is not the tongues you need but the baptism. If you will allow God to baptize you, the other will be all right."

I answered, "My dear sister, I know I am baptized. You know that I have to leave here at four o'clock. Please lay hands on me so that I may receive the tongues."

She stood up and laid her hands on me, and the fire fell.

There came a persistent knock at the door, and she had to go out. That was the best thing that could have happened, for I was alone with God. Then He gave me a revelation. Oh, it was wonderful! He showed me an empty cross and Jesus glorified. I do thank God that the cross is empty, that Christ is no longer on the cross.

Then I saw that God had purified me. I was conscious of the cleaning of the precious blood of Jesus, and I cried out, "Clean! Clean! Clean!" I was filled with the joy of the consciousness of the cleansing. As I was extolling, glorifying, and praising Him, I was speaking in tongues *"as the Spirit gave* [me] *utterance"* (Acts 2:4). I knew then that I had received the real baptism in the Holy Spirit.

It was all as beautiful and peaceful as when Jesus said, *"Peace, be still!"* (Mark 4:39). The tranquillity and the joy of that moment surpassed anything I had ever known up to that time. But hallelujah! These days have grown with greater, mightier, more wonderful divine manifestations and power. That was only the beginning. There is no end to this kind of beginning. You will never come to the end of the Holy Spirit until you have arrived in glory—until you are right in the presence of God forever. And even then we will always be conscious of His presence.

What had I received? I had received the biblical evidence. This biblical evidence is wonderful to me. I knew I had received the very evidence of the Spirit's incoming that the apostles had received on the Day of Pentecost. I knew that everything I had had up to that time was in the nature of an anointing, bringing me in line with God in preparation. However, now I knew I had the biblical baptism in the Spirit. It had the backing of the Scriptures. You are never right if you do not have a foundation for your testimony in the Word of God.

For many years, I have thrown out a challenge to any person who can prove to me that he has the baptism without the speaking in tongues as the Spirit gives utterance—to prove it by the Word that he has been baptized in the Holy Spirit without the biblical evidence—but so far, no one has accepted the challenge. I only say this because so many are like I was; they have a rigid idea that they have received the baptism, without having the biblical evidence. The Lord Jesus wants those who preach the Word to have the Word in evidence. Don't be misled by anything else. Have a biblical proof for everything you have, and then you will be in a place where no man can move you.

When I returned home from Sunderland, my wife said to me, "So you think you have received the baptism of the Holy Spirit? Why, I am as much baptized in the Holy Spirit as you are." We had sat on the platform together for twenty years, but that night she said, "Tonight you will go by yourself." I said, "All right." My wife went back to one of the furthermost seats in the hall, and she said to herself, "I will watch it."

As I went up to the platform that night, the Lord gave me the first few verses of the sixty-first chapter of Isaiah, starting with the first verse:

Biblical Evidence of the Baptism

The Spirit of the Lord GOD is upon Me, be-
cause the LORD has anointed Me to preach
good tidings to the poor; He has sent Me to
heal the brokenhearted, to proclaim liberty to
the captives, and the opening of the prison to
those who are bound.   *(v. 1)*

I preached that night on the subject the Lord had given me, and I told what the Lord had done for me. I told the people that I was going to have God in my life and that I would gladly suffer a thousand deaths rather than forfeit this wonderful infilling that had come to me.

My wife was very restless, just as if she were sitting on a red-hot poker. She was moved in a new way and said, "That is not my Smith that is preaching. Lord, You have done something for him."

As soon as I finished, the secretary of the mission got up and said, "I want what the leader of our mission has got." He tried to sit down but missed his seat and fell on the floor. There were soon fourteen of them on the floor, my own wife included. We did not know what to do, but the Holy Spirit got hold of the situation, and the fire fell. A revival started and the crowds came. It was only the beginning of the flood tide of blessing. We had touched the reservoir of the Lord's life and power. Since that time, the Lord has taken me to many different lands, and I have witnessed many blessed outpourings of God's Holy Spirit.

THREE WITNESSES TO THE BAPTISM

I want to take you to the Scriptures to prove my position that tongues are the evidence of the baptism in the Holy Spirit. Businessmen know that in cases of law where there are two clear witnesses, they could win a case before any judge. On the clear evidence of two witnesses, any judge will give a verdict. What has God given us? He has given us three clear witnesses on the baptism in the Holy Spirit—more than are necessary in law courts.

The first is in Acts 2:4, on the Day of Pentecost:

They were all filled with the Holy Spirit and began to speak with other tongues, as the Spirit gave them utterance.

Here we have the original pattern. And God gave to Peter an eternal word that couples this experience with the promise that came before it: *"This is what was spoken by the prophet Joel"* (v. 16). God wants you to have this—nothing less than this. He wants you to receive the baptism in the Holy Spirit according to this original Pentecostal pattern.

In Acts 10, we have another witness. Cornelius had had a vision of a holy angel and had sent for Peter. When Peter arrived and proclaimed the Gospel message, the Holy Spirit fell on all those who heard his words.

A person said to me one day, "You don't admit that I am filled and baptized with the Holy Spirit. Why, I was ten days and ten nights on my back before the Lord, and He was flooding my soul with joy." I said, "Praise the Lord, sister, that was only the beginning. The disciples were waiting for that length of time, and the mighty power of God fell upon them. The Bible tells us what happened when the power fell." And that is just what happened in the house of Cornelius. The Holy Spirit fell on all those who heard the Word.

And those of the circumcision who believed were astonished, as many as came with Peter, because the gift of the Holy Spirit had been poured out on the Gentiles also.   (Acts 10:45)

What convinced these prejudiced Jews that the Holy Spirit had come? *"For they heard them speak with tongues and magnify God"* (v. 46). There was no other way for them to know. This evidence could not be contradicted. It is the biblical evidence.

If some people were to have an angel come and talk to them as Cornelius did, they would say that they knew they were baptized. Do not be fooled by anything. Be sure that what you receive is according to the Word of God.

We have heard two witnesses. Now let us look at Acts 19:6, which records Paul ministering to certain disciples in Ephesus:

And when Paul had laid hands on them, the Holy Spirit came upon them, and they spoke with tongues and prophesied.

These Ephesians received the identical biblical evidence that the apostles had received at the beginning, and they prophesied in addition. Three times the Scriptures show us this evidence of the baptism in the Spirit. I do not glorify tongues. No, by God's grace, I glorify the Giver of tongues. And above all, I glorify Him whom the Holy Spirit has come to reveal to us, the Lord Jesus Christ. It is He who sends the

Holy Spirit, and I glorify Him because He makes no distinction between us and those who believed at the beginning.

But what are tongues for? Look at the second verse of 1 Corinthians 14, and you will see a very blessed truth. Oh, hallelujah! Have you been there, beloved? I tell you, God wants to take you there. *"For he who speaks in a tongue does not speak to men but to God, for no one understands him; however, in the spirit he speaks mysteries."* The passage goes on to say, *"He who speaks in a tongue edifies himself"* (v. 4).

Enter into the promises of God. It is your inheritance. You will do more in one year if you are really filled with the Holy Spirit than you could do in fifty years apart from Him. I pray that you may be so filled with Him that it will not be possible for you to move without a revival of some kind resulting.

5

Paul's Conversion
and Baptism

aul was probably the greatest persecutor
that the early church had. Saul hated the
Christians: *"He made havoc of the church,
entering every house, and dragging off men
and women, committing them to prison"* (Acts 8:3).
In Acts 9, we read that he was breathing out threats
and slaughter against the disciples of the Lord. He
was on his way to Damascus for the purpose of destroying the church there (vv. 1–2).

How did God deal with such a person? We would
have dealt with him in judgment. God dealt with
him in mercy. Oh, the wondrous love of God! He
loved the believers at Damascus, and the way He
preserved them was through the salvation of the
man who intended to scatter and destroy them. Our
God delights to be merciful, and His grace is granted
daily to both sinner and saint. He shows mercy to
all. If we would just realize that we are alive today
only through the grace of our God.

More and more, I see that it is through the grace of God that I am preserved every day. It is when we realize the goodness of God that we are brought to repentance. Here was Saul, with letters from the high priest, hurrying to Damascus. He was struck down, and he saw a light, a light that was brighter than the sun. As he fell speechless to the ground, he heard a voice saying to him, *"Saul, Saul, why are you persecuting Me?"* He asked, *"Who are You, Lord?"* And the answer came back, *"I am Jesus, whom you are persecuting."* And Saul cried, *"Lord, what do You want me to do?"* (Acts 9:4–6).

I do not want to bring any word of condemnation to anyone, but I know that there are many who have felt very much the same way toward the children of God as Paul did, especially toward those who have received the Pentecostal baptism. I know that many people tell us, "You are mad," but the truth is that the children of God are the only people who are really glad. We are glad inside and we are glad outside. Our gladness flows from the inside. God has filled us with *"joy inexpressible and full of glory"* (1 Pet. 1:8). We are so happy about what we have received that, if it were not for the desire to keep a little decorum, we might be doing strange things. This is probably how the apostle Paul felt when he referred to himself and his coworkers as being *"beside* [them]*selves"* (2 Cor. 5:13) in the Lord. This joy in the Holy Spirit is beyond anything else. And this joy of the Lord is our strength (Neh. 8:10).

When Saul went down to Damascus, he thought he would do wonderful things with that bunch of letters he had from the high priest. But I think he dropped them all on the road. If he ever wanted to pick them up, he was not able to, for he lost his sight. The men who were with him lost their speech—they were speechless—but they led him to Damascus.

There are some people who have an idea that it is only preachers who can know the will of God. However, this account of Saul shows us that the Lord had a disciple in Damascus, named Ananias, a man behind the scenes, who lived in a place where God could talk to him. His ears were open. He was one who listened in to the things from heaven. Oh, they are so much more marvelous than anything you can hear on earth. It was to this man that the Lord appeared in a vision. He told him to go down to the street called Straight and to inquire for Saul. And He told him that Saul had seen in a vision a man named Ananias coming in and putting his hand on him so that he might receive his sight. Ananias protested,

> *Lord, I have heard from many about this man, how much harm he has done to Your saints in Jerusalem. And here he has authority from the chief priests to bind all who call on Your name.* (Acts 9:13–14)

But the Lord reassured Ananias that Saul was a chosen vessel, and Ananias, doubting nothing, went on his errand of mercy.

The Lord had told Ananias concerning Saul, *"Behold, he is praying"* (v. 11). Repentant prayer is always heard in heaven. The Lord never despises a broken and contrite heart (Ps. 51:17). Saul was given a vision that was soon to be a reality, the vision of Ananias coming to pray for him so that he would receive his sight.

I was at one time in the city of Belfast. I had been preaching there, and I had a free day. I had received a number of letters and was looking through them. There were about twenty needy cases in that city, cases that I was asked to visit. As I was looking through my letters, a man came up to me and said, "Are you visiting the sick?" He pointed me to a certain house and told me to go to it and there I would see a very sick woman. I went to the house, and I saw a very helpless woman propped up in bed. I knew that, humanly speaking, she was beyond all help. She was breathing with short, sharp breaths, as if every breath would be her last.

I cried to the Lord and said, "Lord, tell me what to do." The Lord said to me, "Read the fifty-third chapter of Isaiah." I opened my Bible and did as I was told. I read down to the fifth verse of this chapter, when all of a sudden, the woman shouted, "I am healed! I am healed!" I was amazed at this sudden exclamation and asked her to tell me what had happened. She said, "Two weeks ago, I was cleaning house, and I strained my heart very badly. Two physicians have been to see me, and they both told me there was no help. But last night, the Lord gave me a vision. I saw you come right into my bedroom. I saw you praying. I saw you open your Bible to the fifty-third chapter of Isaiah. When you got down to the fifth verse and read the words, *'By His stripes we are healed,'* I saw myself wonderfully healed. That was a vision; now it is a fact."

Paul's Conversion and Baptism

I do thank God that visions have not ceased. The Holy Spirit can give visions, and we may expect them in these last days. God does not will the death of any sinner (Ezek. 33:11), and He will use all kinds of means for their salvation. I do praise God for this Gospel. It is always so entreating. *"Look to Me, and be saved, all you ends of the earth!"* (Isa. 45:22) is such an inviting message. Oh, what a Gospel! Whatever people say about it, it is surely a message of love.

Ananias went down to the house on Straight Street, and he laid his hands on the one who had before been a blasphemer and a persecutor, and he said to him, *"Brother Saul, the Lord Jesus, who appeared to you on the road as you came, has sent me that you may receive your sight and be filled with the Holy Spirit"* (Acts 9:17). He recognized him as a brother whose soul had already been saved and who had come into relationship with the Father and with all the family of God, but there was something necessary beyond this. Yes, the Lord had not forgotten his physical condition, and there was healing for him. But there was something beyond this. It was the filling with the Holy Spirit.

Oh, it always seems to me that the Gospel is robbed of its divine glory when we overlook this marvelous truth of the baptism of the Holy Spirit. To be saved is wonderful; to be a new creature, to have passed from death to life, to have the witness of the Spirit that you are born of God—all this is unspeakably precious. But whereas we have the well of salvation bubbling up inside us, we need to go on to a place where from within us will flow *"rivers of living water"* (John 7:38). The Lord Jesus showed us very plainly that, if we believe in Him, from within us will flow these *"rivers of living water."* And this He spoke by the Spirit. The Lord wants us to be filled with the Spirit, to have the manifestation of the presence of His Spirit, the manifestation that is indeed given *"for the profit of all"* (1 Cor. 12:7). The Lord wants us to be His mouthpieces and to speak as the very oracles of God.

God chose Saul. What was he? A blasphemer. A persecutor. That is grace. Our God is gracious, and He loves to show His mercy to the vilest and worst of men.

There was a notable character in the town in which I lived who was known as the worst man in town. He was so vile, and his language was so horrible, that even wicked men could not stand it. In England, they have what is known as the public hangman who has to perform all the executions. This man held that appointment, and he told me later that he believed that when he performed the execution of men who had committed murder, the demon power that was in them would come upon him, and that, in consequence, he had been possessed by a legion of demons.

His life was so miserable that he decided to kill himself. He went down to a certain train depot and purchased a ticket. English trains are much different from American trains. In every coach there are a number of small compartments, and it is easy for anyone who wants to commit suicide to open the door of his compartment and throw himself out of the train. This man purposed to throw himself out of the train in a certain tunnel just as the train coming from the opposite direction would be about to dash past; he thought this would make a quick end to his life.

There was a young man at the depot that night who had been saved the night before. He was all on fire to get others saved, and he purposed in his heart that every day of his life, he would get someone saved. He saw this dejected hangman and began to speak to him about his soul. He brought him down to our mission, and there he came under a mighty conviction of sin. For two-and-a-half hours he was literally sweating under conviction, and you could see a vapor rising up from him. At the end of two-and-a-half hours, he was graciously saved.

I said, "Lord, tell me what to do." The Lord said, "Don't leave him. Go home with him." I went to his house. When he saw his wife, he said, "God has saved me." The wife broke down, and she too was graciously saved. I tell you, there was a difference in that home. Even the cat knew the difference. Previous to this, the cat would always run away when that hangman came through the door. But the night that he was saved, the cat jumped onto his knee and went to sleep.

There were two sons in that house, and one of them said to his mother, "Mother, what is up in our house? It was never like this before. It is so peaceful. What is it?" She told him, "Father has gotten saved." The other son was also struck by the change.

I took this man to many special services, and the power of God was on him for many days. He would give his testimony, and as he grew in grace, he desired to preach the Gospel. He became an evangelist, and hundreds and hundreds were brought to a saving knowledge of the Lord Jesus Christ through his ministry. The grace of God is sufficient for the vilest, and He can take the most wicked men and make them monuments of His grace. He did this with Saul of Tarsus at the very time he was breathing out threats and slaughter against the disciples of the Lord. He did it with Berry the hangman. He will do it for hundreds more in response to our cries.

You will notice that when Ananias came into that house, he called the onetime enemy of the Gospel *"Brother Saul"* (Acts 9:17). He recognized that in those three days a blessed work had been accomplished and that Saul had been brought into relationship with the Father and with the Lord Jesus Christ. Was this not enough? No, there was something further, and for this purpose the Lord had sent Ananias to that house. The Lord Jesus had sent him to that house to put his hands upon this newly saved brother so that he might receive his sight and be filled with the Holy Spirit.

You say, "But it does not say that he spoke in tongues." We know that Paul did speak in tongues, that he spoke in tongues more than all the Corinthians (1 Cor. 14:18). In those early days, it was so soon after the time of that first Pentecostal outpouring that they would never have been satisfied with anyone receiving the baptism unless he received it according to the original pattern given on the Day of Pentecost.

When Peter was relating what had taken place in the house of Cornelius at Caesarea, he said, *"As I began to speak, the Holy Spirit fell upon them, as upon us at the beginning"* (Acts 11:15). Later, speaking of this incident, he said,

Paul's Conversion and Baptism

God, who knows the heart, acknowledged them
by giving them the Holy Spirit, just as He did
to us, and made no distinction between us and
them, purifying their hearts by faith.
(Acts 15:8–9)

We know from the account of what took place at Cornelius's household that when the Holy Spirit fell, *"they heard them speak with tongues and magnify God"* (Acts 10:46).

Many people think that God makes a distinction between us and those who lived at the beginning of the church. But they have no Scripture for this. When anyone receives the gift of the Holy Spirit, there will assuredly be no difference between his experience today and what was given on the Day of Pentecost. And I cannot believe that, when Saul was filled with the Holy Spirit, the Lord made any difference in the experience that Ho gave him than the experience that He had given to Peter and the rest a short while before.

And so Saul was filled with the Holy Spirit, and in the later chapters of the Acts of the Apostles we see the result of this infilling. Oh, what a difference it makes.

The grace of God that was given to the persecuting Saul is available for you. The same infilling of the Holy Spirit that he received is likewise available. Do not rest satisfied with any lesser experience than the baptism that the disciples received on the Day of Pentecost. Then move on to a life of continuous receiving of more and more of the blessed Spirit of God.

6

Receiving the Baptism

I believe God wants us to know more about the baptism of the Holy Spirit. And I believe that God wants us to know the truth in such a way that we may all have a clear understanding of what He means when He desires all His people to receive the Holy Spirit.

I want you to read this passage from the first chapter of the Acts of the Apostles:

The former account I made, O Theophilus, of all that Jesus began both to do and teach, until the day in which He was taken up, after He through the Holy Spirit had given commandments to the apostles whom He had chosen, to whom He also presented Himself alive after His suffering by many infallible proofs, being seen by them during forty days and speaking of the things pertaining to the kingdom of God. And being assembled together with them, He commanded them not to depart from Jerusalem, but to wait for the Promise of the Father, "which," He said, "you have heard from

*Me; for John truly baptized with water, but
you shall be baptized with the Holy Spirit not
many days from now." Therefore, when they
had come together, they asked Him, saying,
"Lord, will You at this time restore the kingdom to Israel?" And He said to them, "It is not
for you to know times or seasons which the Father has put in His own authority. But you
shall receive power when the Holy Spirit has
come upon you; and you shall be witnesses to
Me in Jerusalem, and in all Judea and Sa-
maria, and to the end of the earth." Now when
He had spoken these things, while they
watched, He was taken up, and a cloud received Him out of their sight. And while they
looked steadfastly toward heaven as He went
up, behold, two men stood by them in white
apparel, who also said, "Men of Galilee, why
do you stand gazing up into heaven? This
same Jesus, who was taken up from you into
heaven, will so come in like manner as you
saw Him go into heaven."* (vv. 1–11)

Jesus, our Mediator and Advocate, was filled
with the Holy Spirit. He commanded His followers
concerning these days we are in and gave instruc-
tions about the time through the Holy Spirit. I can
see that if we are going to accomplish anything, we
are going to accomplish it because we are under the
power of the Holy Spirit.

During my lifetime, I have seen lots of satanic
forces, Spiritualists, and all other "ists." I tell you
that there is a power that is satanic, and there is a
power that is the Holy Spirit. I remember that after

we received the Holy Spirit and when people were speaking in tongues as the Spirit gave utterance—we don't know the Holy Spirit in any other way—the Spiritualists heard about it and came to the meeting in good time to fill two rows of seats.

When the power of God fell upon us, these imitators began their shaking and moving, with utterances from the satanic forces. The Spirit of the Lord was mighty upon me. I went to them and said, "Now you demons, clear out of here!" And out they went. I followed them right out into the street, and then they turned around and cursed me. It made no difference; they were out.

Beloved, the Lord wants us to know in these days that there is a fullness of God where all other powers must cease to be. And I implore you to hear that the baptism in the Holy Spirit is to possess us so that we are, and may be continually, so full of the Holy Spirit that utterances and revelations and eyesight and everything else may be so remarkably controlled by the Spirit of God that we live and move in this glorious sphere of usefulness for the glory of God.

And I believe that God wants to help us to see that every child of God ought to receive the Holy Spirit. Beloved, God wants us to understand that this is not difficult when we are in the right order. And I want you to see what it means to seek the Holy Spirit.

If we were to examine John's gospel, we would see that Jesus predicted all that we are getting today with the coming of the Holy Spirit. Our Lord said that the Holy Spirit would take of the things of His

Word and reveal them to us. (See John 14:26; 16:14.) He would live out in us all of the life of Jesus.

If we could only think of what this really means! It is one of the ideals. Talk about graduation! My word! Come into the graduation of the Holy Spirit, and you will simply outstrip everything they have in any college there ever was. You would leave them all behind, just as I have seen the sun leave the mist behind in San Francisco. You would leave what is as cold as ice and go into the sunshine.

God the Holy Spirit wants us to know the reality of this fullness of the Spirit so that we will neither be ignorant nor have mystic conceptions but will have a clear, unmistakable revelation of the entire mind of God for these days.

Interpretation of Tongues

The Spirit of the living God comes with such divine revelation, such unveiling about Him, such a clearness of what He was to the people, and He brings within us the breath of that eternal power that makes us know we are right here, this very hour, to carry out His plan for now and what God will have for the future, for there is no limitation but rather an enforcement of character, of clearness of vision, of an openness of countenance until we behold Him in every divine light.

Glory! Oh, it is grand! Thank God for that interpretation.

I implore you, beloved, in the name of Jesus, that you should see that you come right into all the mind of God. Jesus truly said, *"But you shall receive*

power when the Holy Spirit has come upon you"
(Acts 1:8). And I want you to know that *"He also
presented Himself alive after His suffering by many
infallible proofs, being seen by them during forty
days"* (v. 3). He is all the time unfolding to every one
of us the power of resurrection.

THE BAPTISM IS RESURRECTION

Remember that the baptism of the Holy Spirit is
resurrection. If you can touch this ideal of God with
its resurrection power, you will see that nothing
earthly can remain; you will see that all disease will
clear out. If you get filled with the Holy Spirit, all
satanic forces that cause fits, all these lame legs, all
these foot afflictions, all these kidney troubles, and
all these nervous, fearful things will go. *Resurrection*
is the word for it. Resurrection shakes away death
and breathes life in you; it lets you know that you
are quickened from the dead by the Spirit and that
you are made like Jesus. Glory to God!

Oh, the word *resurrection!* I wish I could say it
on the same level as the word *Jesus.* They very har-
moniously go together. Jesus is resurrection, and to
know Jesus in this resurrection power is simply to
see that you no longer have to be dead; you are alive
unto God by the Spirit.

ENTERING INTO A NEW REALM

If you are a businessman, you need to be baptized
in the Holy Spirit. For any kind of business, you need
to know the power of the Holy Spirit, because if you

are not baptized with the Holy Spirit, Satan has a tremendous power to interfere with the progress of your life. If you come into the baptism of the Holy Spirit, there is a new realm for your business.

I remember one day being in London at a meeting. About eleven o'clock, they said to me, "We will have to close the meeting. We are not allowed to have this place any later than eleven o'clock." There were several who were under the power of the Spirit. A man rose up and looked at me, saying, "Oh, don't leave me, please. I feel that I do not dare be left. I must receive the Holy Spirit. Will you go home with us?" "Yes," I said, "I will go." His wife was there as well. They were two hungry people just being awakened by the power of the Spirit to know that they were lacking in their lives and that they needed the power of God.

In about an hour's time, we arrived at their big, beautiful house in the country. It was wintertime. He began stirring the fire up and putting coal on, and he said, "We will soon have a tremendous fire, so we will get warmed. Then we will have a big supper." And I suppose the next thing would have been going to bed.

"No, thank you," I said. "I have not come here for your supper or for your bed. I thought you wanted me to come with you so that you might receive the Holy Spirit."

"Oh," he replied. "Will you pray with us?"

"I have come for nothing else." I knew I could keep myself warm in a prayer meeting without a fire.

About half past three in the morning, his wife was as full as could be, speaking in tongues. God was doing wonderful things that night. I went to the end of the table. There he was, groaning terribly. So I said, "Your wife has received the Holy Spirit." "Oh," he said, "this is going to be a big night for me." I tell you, you also will have big nights like this man had, whether you receive the baptism or not, if you will seek God with all your heart.

I often say there is more done in the seeking than in any other way. In the Scriptures, there is no such thing as seeking for the Holy Spirit. But we have to get to a place where we know that unless we meet face to face with God and get all the crooked places out of our lives, there will be no room for the Holy Spirit, for the indwelling presence of God. But when God gets a chance at us, and by the vision of the blood of Jesus we see ourselves as God sees us, then we have a revelation. Without this, we are undone and helpless.

At five o'clock in the morning, this man stood up and said, "I am through." He was not baptized. "I am settled," he continued. "God has settled me. Now I must have a few hours' rest before I go to my business at eight o'clock."

My word! That was quite a day at his business. In many years, he had never lived a day like that. He went about his business among all his men, and they said, "What is up with the man? What is up with the boss? What has taken place? Oh, what a change!"

The whole place was electrified. God had turned the lion into the lamb. Oh, formerly he had been like a great big lion prowling about, but God had touched him. The touch of Omnipotence had broken this man down until right there in his business the men were broken up in his presence. Oh, I tell you, there is something in pursuing; there is something in waiting. What is it? It is this: God slays a man so that he may begin on a new plane in his life. We will have to be utterly slain if we want to know that resurrection power of Jesus.

That night, at about ten o'clock, he was baptized in the Holy Spirit in a meeting. A short time afterward, when I was passing through the grounds toward this man's house, his two sons rushed out to where I was, threw their arms around me, and kissed me, saying, "You have sent us a new father."

Oh, the power of the Holy Spirit creates new men and new women. The Holy Spirit takes away your stony heart and gives you a heart of flesh (Ezek. 36:26–27). And when God gets His way like that, there is a tremendous shaking among the dry bones (see Ezekiel 37:4–10), for God gets His way with the people.

We must see that we are no good unless God takes charge of us. But when He gets real charge of us, what a plan for the future! What a wonderful open door for God!

Oh, beloved, we must see this ideal by the Spirit! What should we do? We do not dare to do anything but go through and receive the baptism. Submit to the power of God. If you yield, other people are saved. You will die unless you have a power of resurrection, a touch for others. But if you live only for God, then other people will be raised out of death and all kinds of evil into a blessed life through the Spirit.

Beloved, we must see that this baptism of the Spirit is greater than everything. You can talk as you like, say what you like, do as you like, but until you have the Holy Spirit, you won't know what the resurrection touch is. Resurrection is by the power of the Spirit. And remember, when I talk about resurrection, I am talking about one of the greatest things in the Scriptures. Resurrection is evidence that we have awakened with a new line of truth that cannot cease to be, but will always go on with a greater force and increasing power with God.

Interpretation of Tongues

Hallelujah! The Spirit breathes, the Spirit lifts, the Spirit renews, the Spirit quickens. He brings life where death was. He brings truth where no vision was. He brings revelation, for God is in that man. He is in the power of the Spirit, lost, hidden, clothed, filled, and resurrected.

Hallelujah! Thank God for that. See to it that today you press on with a new order of the Spirit so that you can never be where you were before. This is a new day for us all. You say, "What about the people who are already baptized in the Spirit?" Oh, this is a new day also for those who have been baptized, for the Spirit is an unlimited source of power. He is in no way stationary. Nothing in God is stationary. God has no place for a person who is stationary. The man who is going to catch the fire, hold forth the truth, and always be on the watchtower, is the one who is going to be a beacon for all saints, having a light greater than he would have naturally. He must see that God's grace, God's life, and God's Spirit are a million times mightier than he.

The man who is baptized in the Holy Spirit is baptized into a new order altogether. You cannot ever be ordinary after that. You are on an extraordinary plane; you are brought into line with the mind of God. You have come into touch with ideals in every way.

If you want oratory, it is in the baptism of the Spirit. If you want the touch of quickened sense that moves your body until you know that you are completely renewed, it is by the Holy Spirit. And while I say so much about the Holy Spirit, I withdraw everything that doesn't put Jesus in the place He belongs. For when I speak about the Holy Spirit, it is always with reference to revelations of Jesus. The Holy Spirit is only the Revealer of the mighty Christ who has everything for us so that we may never know any weakness. All limitations are gone. And you are now in a place where God has taken the ideal and moved you on with His own velocity, which has a speed beyond all human mind and thought. Glory to God!

Interpretation of Tongues
Wake, you who sleep, and allow the Lord to wake you into righteousness. The liberty with which God has set you free—God has made you free to enlarge others who are bound.

So the Spirit of the Lord must have His way in everything. Oh, what would happen if we would all loosen ourselves up! Sometimes I think it is almost necessary to give an address to those who are already baptized in the Holy Spirit. I feel that, just like the Corinthian church, we may have, as it were, gifts and graces, and we may use them all, but we sit in them and do not go on beyond where we are.

I maintain that all gifts and graces are only for one thing: to make you desire gifts and graces. Don't miss what I say. Every touch of the divine life by the Spirit is only for one purpose: to make your life go on to a higher height than where you are. Beloved, if anybody has to rise up in the meeting to tell me how they were baptized with the Holy Spirit in order for me to know they are baptized, I say, "You have fallen from grace. You ought to have such a baptism that everybody can tell you are baptized without your telling how you were baptized." That would make a new day. That would be a sermon in itself to everybody, not only in here but also outside. Then people would follow you to get to know where you have come from and where you are going. (See John 3:8.) You say, "I want that. I won't settle until I get that." God will surely give it to you.

The Holy Spirit never comes until there is a place ready for Him. The Holy Spirit can only come into us (His temples) when we are fully yielded to Him, for the Spirit *"does not dwell in temples made with hands"* (Acts 7:48) but in *"tablets of flesh, that is, of the heart"* (2 Cor. 3:3). So it doesn't matter what kind of a building you get; you cannot count on the building being a substitute for the Holy Spirit. You will all have to be temples of the Holy Spirit for the building to be anything like Holy Spirit order.

The Holy Spirit could not come until the apostles and the other disciples who were in the Upper Room on the Day of Pentecost were all of one mind and heart, all of one accord with each other and with God. Let me quote one verse to help you, because I am talking about the truth of what the fullness of *"the latter rain"* (Zech. 10:1) and the rapture of the church mean. James 5:7 is a beautiful verse regarding these things:

Smith Wigglesworth on the Holy Spirit

*Therefore be patient, brethren, until the com-
ing of the Lord. See how the farmer waits for
the precious fruit of the earth.*

What is the precious fruit of the earth? Is it cab-
bages? Is it grapes? The precious fruit of the earth is
the church, the body of Christ. And God has no
thought for other things. He causes the vegetation of
the earth to grow and creates the glory of the flower.
He gives attention to the beauty of flowers because
He knows it will please us. But when speaking about
the precious fruit of the earth, our Lord has His
mind upon you today, and He says,

*See how the farmer waits for the precious fruit
of the earth, waiting patiently for it until it receives the early and latter rain. You also be patient. Establish your hearts, for the coming of
the Lord is at hand.   (James 5:7–8)*

So if you desire the coming of the Lord, you
must certainly advocate having every believer filled
with the Holy Spirit. The more a man is filled with
the Holy Spirit, the more he will be ready to forecast
the return of the Lord and send forth this glorious
truth.

The Holy Spirit cannot come until the church is
ready. And you say, "When will the church be
ready?" If believers were in an attitude of yieldedness and were in unity with God and each other, God
could send the breath right now to make the church
ready in ten minutes, even less than that.

So we can clearly say that the coming of the
Lord is near to us, but it will be even closer to us as

we are ready to receive a fuller and greater manifestation. What will be the manifestation of the coming of the Lord? If we were ready, and if the power of God were stressing that truth today, we would be rushing up to one another, saying, "He is coming; I know He is coming." "He is coming!" "Yes, I know He is." Every person around would be saying, "He is coming," and you would know He is coming.

That is the only hope of the future, and there is nothing except the Holy Spirit that can prepare the hearts of the people to rush up and down and say, "He is coming. He is coming soon." Praise God, He will come as surely as we are in this place. He is coming!

ALLOW GOD TO USE YOU

There are things I have had to learn about the baptism.

One day, in England, a lady wrote to ask if I would come and help her. She said she was blind, having two blood clots behind her eyes. I had been in London recently, and I didn't feel I wanted to go. However, I sent a letter, not knowing who she was, saying that if she was willing to go into a room with me and shut the door and never come out until she had perfect sight, I would come. She sent word, "Oh, come!"

The moment I reached the house, they brought in this blind woman. After we shook hands, she made her way to a room, opened the door, allowed me to go in, and then came in and shut the door. "Now," she said, "we are with God."

Have you ever been there? It is a lovely place.

In an hour and a half, the power of God fell upon us. Rushing to the window, she exclaimed, "I can see! Oh, I can see! The blood is gone; I can see!" Sitting down in a chair, she asked, "Could I receive the Holy Spirit?"

"Yes," I replied, "if all is right with God."

"You don't know me," she continued, "but for ten years I have been fighting your position. I couldn't bear these tongues, but God settled it today. I want the baptism of the Holy Spirit."

After she had prayed and repented of what she had said about tongues, she was filled with the Holy Spirit and began speaking in tongues.

When you put your hands upon people to pray, you can tell when the Holy Spirit is present. And if you will only yield to the Holy Spirit and allow Him to move, my word, what will happen!

RECEIVE THE SPIRIT AS A CHILD

I wonder how many people there are today who are prepared to be baptized? Oh, you say you couldn't be baptized? Then you have been an adult too long. You need to become childlike again. Do you know that there is a difference between being a baby and anything else in the world? Many people have been waiting for years for the baptism, and what has been the problem? We are told in the Scriptures,

> *At that time Jesus answered and said, "I thank You, Father, Lord of heaven and earth, that You have hidden these things from the*

*wise and prudent and have revealed them to
babes."*   *(Matt. 11:25)*

What is the wise man's difficulty? A wise man is
too careful. And while he is in the operation of the
Spirit, he wants to know what he is saying. No man
can know what he is saying when the Spirit is upon
him. His own mind is inactive. If you get into that
place in which you are near God, your mind is entirely obliterated, and the mind of Christ comes by
the power of the Spirit. Under these conditions,
Christ prays and speaks in the Spirit through you as
the Spirit gives utterance.

It is the mind and plan of God for us to receive
the Holy Spirit. What is the difference between the
"wise and prudent" man and a baby? If you will get
childlike enough this afternoon, at least fifty people
will be baptized in the Holy Spirit. If you will only
yield to God and let the Spirit have His way, God
will fill you with the Holy Spirit.

In Sweden, the power of God was upon us, and I
believe that more than a hundred people received
the Holy Spirit in a quarter of an hour. May God
grant it this afternoon. Beloved, it will be so, for God
is with us.

The natural man cannot receive the Spirit of God
(1 Cor. 2:14). But when you get into a supernatural
place, then you receive the mind of God. Again, what
is the difference between a *"wise and prudent"* man
and a baby? The man drinks cautiously, but the baby
swallows it all, and the mother has to hold the bottle,
or some of that will go down, too. This is how God
wants it to be in the Spirit: The spiritually-minded
baby cannot walk. However, God walks in him. The

spiritually-minded baby cannot talk, but God talks through him. The spiritually-minded baby cannot dress himself, but God dresses him and clothes him with His righteousness.

Oh, beloved, if we can only be infants in this way today, great things will take place along the lines and thought of the Spirit of God. The Lord wants us all to be so like-minded with Him that He can put His seal upon us.

There are some in this meeting who no doubt have never been saved. Where the saints are seeking, and leaving themselves to the operation of the Spirit, there will be newborn children in the midst. God will save in our midst. God will use this means of blessing if we will only let ourselves go. You say, "What can I do?" The fiddler will drop his fiddle, the drummer his drum. If there is anybody here who has anything hanging around him, weighing him down, it will fall off. If you will become childlike enough today, everything else will fall off, and you will be free. You will be able to run and skip in the street, and you will be happy.

Does the baby ever lose his intelligence? Does he ever lose his common sense? Does the baby who comes into the will of God lose his reason or his credentials in any way? No, God will increase your abilities and help you in everything. I am not talking here about just being a baby. I am talking about being a baby in the Spirit. Paul says in 1 Corinthians 14:20, *"In malice be babes, but in understanding be mature."* And I believe the Spirit would breathe through all the attributes of the Spirit so that we may understand what the mind of the Lord is concerning us in the Holy Spirit.

Receiving the Baptism

Oh, this blessed thought. I want to help all who are being baptized to help others. If you have ever spoken in tongues in your life, let yourself go today, and God will speak through you. You must have a day you have never had before. This must be an ideal day in the Spirit, a day with the anointing of the Spirit, a day with the mind of God in the Spirit.

7

Our Heavenly Dwelling

I believe the Lord would be pleased for us to turn to the fourth chapter of 2 Corinthians and read from the sixteenth verse, concluding with the seventh verse of the fifth chapter:

For which cause we faint not; but though our outward man perish, yet the inward man is renewed day by day. For our light affliction, which is but for a moment, worketh for us a far more exceeding and eternal weight of glory; while we look not at the things which are seen, but at the things which are not seen: for the things which are seen are temporal; but the things which are not seen are eternal. For we know that if our earthly house of this tabernacle were dissolved, we have a building of God, an house not made with hands, eternal in the heavens. For in this we groan, earnestly desiring to be clothed upon with our house which is from heaven: if so be that being

clothed we shall not be found naked. For we that are in this tabernacle do groan, being burdened: not for that we would be unclothed, but clothed upon, that mortality might be swallowed up of life. Now he that hath wrought us for the selfsame thing is God, who also hath given unto us the earnest of the Spirit. Therefore we are always confident, knowing that, whilst we are at home in the body, we are absent from the Lord: (for we walk by faith, not by sight).

(2 Cor. 4:16–5:7 KJV)

I believe the Lord has in His mind the further freedom of life. Nothing will please the Lord so much as for us to come into our fullness of redemption, because I believe that *"the Lord is the Spirit; and where the Spirit of the Lord is, there is liberty"* (2 Cor. 3:17).

WHAT ABOUT MANIFESTATIONS?

Liberty is beautiful when we never use it to satisfy ourselves but use it in the Lord. We must never transgress because of liberty. What I mean is this: it would be wrong for me to take opportunities just because the Spirit of the Lord is upon me. But it would be perfectly justifiable if I clearly allow the Spirit of the Lord to have His liberty with me. However, we are not to behave inappropriately in our liberty, for the flesh is more extravagant than the Spirit.

The Spirit's extravagances are always for edification, strengthening character, and bringing us all more into conformity with the life of Christ. But fleshly extravagances always mar and bring the saints into a place of trial for a moment. As the Spirit of the Lord takes further hold of a person, we may get liberty in it, but we are tried through the manifestations of it.

I believe we have come to a liberty of the Spirit that is so pure it will never bring a frown of distraction over another person's mind. I have seen many people who were in the power of the Spirit and yet exhibited a manifestation that was not foundational or even helpful. I have seen people under the mighty power of the Holy Spirit who have waved their hands wildly and moved on the floor and gone on in such a state that no one could say the body was not under the power. However, there was more natural power than spiritual power there, and the natural condition of the person, along with the spiritual condition, caused the manifestation. Though we know the Spirit of the Lord was there, the manifestation was not something that would elevate or please the people or grant them a desire for more of that. It wasn't an edification of the Spirit.

If there are any here who have those manifestations, I want to help you. I don't want to hurt you. It is good that you should have the Spirit upon you; people need to be filled with the Spirit. But you never have a right to say you couldn't help doing this, that, or the other manifestation.

No manifestation of the body ever glorifies the Lord except the tongue. If you seek to be free in the operation of the Spirit through the mouth, then the tongue, which may be under a kind of subconscious control by the Spirit, brings out the glory of the Lord, and that will always bring edification, consolation, and comfort.

No other manifestation will do this. Still, I believe that it is necessary to have all these other manifestations when someone is filled with the Spirit for the first time. It seems to be almost necessary for some people to kick. I have seen some people leaping in the air so that you could hardly see across the room.

When the Spirit is there, the flesh must find some way out, and so, through past experience, we allow all these things at the beginning. But I believe the Holy Spirit brings a sound condition of mind, and the first thing must pass away so that the divine position may remain. And so there are various manifestations, including kicking and waving, that take place at the incoming of the Holy Spirit, when the flesh and the Spirit are in conflict. One must decrease and die, and the other must increase and multiply.

Consequently, when you come to understand this, you are in a place of sound judgment and know that now the Holy Spirit has come to take you on with God.

Suppose I were to read this Scripture verse in a meeting:

We do not look at the things which are seen, but at the things which are not seen. For the things which are seen are temporary, but the things which are not seen are eternal.
(2 Cor. 4:18)

What would you think if, at this point, I had to stop because of a great kicking sensation, and I had to lie down on the floor for three hours before I could go on with what the Spirit of the Lord was saying because my body and spirit were in disagreement? The glory of the Lord is upon me, and the Lord is speaking through me, but now I must stop to have a half hour of kicking. All the people in the audience are waiting to see Wigglesworth kick through a half hour before he goes on. I wonder if you would think that was in the will of God?

I don't believe it is in the will of God, and I never believe you have a license to do it. I will never believe that God would baptize you with the Holy Spirit and then make you like a machine so that you couldn't begin at any time and stop at any time.

All these things that I am speaking about are necessary for you for further advancement in the Spirit. To me it is a very marvelous thing that the Spirit can have such mightiness over a body to kick out the flesh.

I have known some people, when they have gone through to receiving the baptism in the Holy Spirit, whom God has begun in a new way. When the Lord baptized me with the Holy Spirit, at first there was so much flesh that needed to be done away with that I went all around the dining room on my knees, clapping my hands. I went through it, and at the end of it was tongues. Then I stopped because there was no more kick left. It couldn't go out through my feet when tongues were coming out through my mouth.

When the Holy Spirit is allowed full reign over the operation of human life, He always works out divine wisdom. And when He gets perfect control of a life, the divine source flows through so that all the people may receive edification in the Spirit. If you act foolishly after you have had wisdom taught you, nobody will give you much leeway.

"We then that are strong ought to bear the infirmities of the weak" (Rom. 15:1 KJV). Some who come to these meetings know nothing about the power of the Holy Spirit. They get saved and are quickened, and after the Spirit comes upon them, you will see all these manifestations. In love and grace, you should bear with them as newborn babes in the Spirit and rejoice with them because that is only a beginning to an end. The Lord wouldn't want us to be anything but *"strong in the Lord and in the power of His might"* (Eph. 6:10) to help everyone around us.

LIVING THE ASCENSION LIFE

I want you to keep these four verses primary in your mind throughout the rest of this message:

> *For we know that if our earthly house of this tabernacle were dissolved, we have a building of God, an house not made with hands, eternal in the heavens. For in this we groan, earnestly desiring to be clothed upon with our house which is from heaven: if so be that being clothed we shall not be found naked. For we that are in this tabernacle do groan, being burdened: not for that we would be unclothed, but clothed upon, that mortality might be swallowed up of life.* (2 Cor. 5:1–4 KJV)

I feel I may speak to you with perfect freedom because I believe the Lord is helping us to comprehend a very deep spiritual condition.

In the first place, I believe that we will all grasp the truth that we are not our own (1 Cor. 6:19). In the second place, we belong to a spiritual order; we don't belong to the earth. And not only that, but our minds and our bodies—our whole position through the eternal Spirit—always have to be on the ascending position. To descend is to be conformed. To ascend is to be transformed.

In this transforming condition, we may, by the power of the Spirit, as God gives us revelation, be lifted up into a very blessed state of fellowship with God, of power with God. And in that place of power with God, we will have power over everything else, for to have all power over the earth, we must first have power with God.

We know we are heavenly citizens. We know we have to exit this earth and have been preparing for our exit. Yet while we are on earth, we must live in the place where we groan over everything that binds us from being loosed from the world.

What will hold me? Association will hold me in this present world. I must have no earthly associations—and you know it is as natural to have an earthly association as it is to live. I must hold every earthly association at a distance. It must never tie me or bind me. It must never have any persuasion over me. Hear what the Scripture says: *"Being conformed to His death"* (Phil. 3:10).

What does it mean to conform to the death of Jesus? It leads me to that death of separation to God, of yieldedness, of exchange, where God takes me to Himself and leaves the old nature behind. *"While we do not look at the things which are seen, but at the things which are not seen"* (2 Cor. 4:18).

Then I may grasp some idea of what it will mean if I die to myself. I want us to see, by the grace of God, that the dissolving (see 2 Corinthians 5:1 KJV) is a great thought. There is a position in God that we must clearly understand: *"Not because we want to be unclothed, but further clothed, that mortality may be swallowed up by life"* (2 Cor. 5:4).

"Mortality" is a great word. While it is necessary, it is a hindrance. While mortality has done a great deal to produce everything we see, it is a hindrance if we live in it. It is a helpful position if we live over it.

Then I must understand how mortality can be *"swallowed up."* I must know how the old body, the old tendencies to the fallen nature, may be swallowed up. There is a verse we must come to. It would serve us to look at it now: *"Always carrying about in the body the dying of the Lord Jesus, that the life of Jesus also may be manifested in our body"* (2 Cor. 4:10).

What is this *"dying of the Lord"*? It is dying to desire. In the measure that we look to one another for our help, we lose faith in God. If you rely upon any man or woman, upon any human assistance, to help you, you fall out of the greater purpose God has for you.

You must learn that no earthly source can ever assist you in this. You are going to this realm of life only by mortality being swallowed up by life: *"And the life which I now live in the flesh I live by faith in the Son of God"* (Gal. 2:20). It is a process of dying and living.

God will help us today. I know He will. I believe that the Lord will not let the preacher be anything anymore. All these messages that God is giving me show me that I have nothing in myself. But thank God, I am in Christ. Truly so.

I do not dare give way to my own self because I would only look like a fool. But I tell you, this life I am speaking about absolutely ravishes you. It absolutely severs you from earthly connections. It absolutely disjoins you from all earthly help. And I can understand this word now more than ever: *"You have not yet resisted to bloodshed, striving against sin"* (Heb. 12:4).

The great striving to the point of bloodshed—blood being the very essence of life—we have not yet resisted to that degree, but we will. I know the Scripture says we have not, but I know it means that we have not arrived there yet. But thank God, we are in it in a measure.

The apostle Paul could see that if he had any communion with flesh and blood, he couldn't go forward in the Lord. (See Galatians 1:15–17.) It was even necessary for Jesus' flesh and blood ties to be put in this context. Jesus said,

"Who is My mother and who are My brothers?" And He stretched out His hand toward His disciples and said, "Here are My mother and My brothers! For whoever does the will of My Father in heaven is My brother and sister and mother." *(Matt. 12:48–50)*

Flesh and blood were nothing to Jesus. The body that brought Him forth was nothing to Him. God brought Him into the world as a seed of life. To Him, that obedient believer was His mother, that servant of God was His brother, that follower of Christ was His sister. But this is a higher ideal; this takes spiritual knowledge.

Let us look at another example of dying to self taken from Jesus' life. In the Garden of Gethsemane,

Jesus faced His suffering from two different stand-points. His human nature instantly cried out, *"If it is possible, let this cup pass from Me"* (Matt. 26:39). The next moment, he was saying, with His divine nature, *"Nevertheless, not as I will, but as You will"* (v. 39). He also said, *"But for this purpose I came to this hour"* (John 12:27). His human nature had no more choices left. He was off to face the cross.

When God the Holy Spirit brings us to see these truths, we will deny ourselves for the sake of the Cross. We will deny ourselves of anything that would cause our brother to stumble. We will die to all fleshly indulgences, lest we should miss the great swallowing up by life (2 Cor. 5:4). We will not even mention or ever pay attention to anything along natural lines.

If we will allow God to govern us, He will lift us up into a higher state of grace than we have ever been in before. If believers could take hold of this spiritual power, they could stand anything along the lines of ridicule by a husband or wife. When are we distracted and disturbed? When we don't reach the ideals in the Spirit. When we reach the ideals in the Spirit, what does it matter? I find that the power of God sanctifies husband and wife.

One half of the trouble in the assemblies is the people's murmuring over the conditions they are in. The Bible teaches us not to murmur. If you reach that standard, you will never murmur anymore. You will be above murmuring. You will be in the place where God is absolutely the exchanger of thought, the exchanger of actions, and the exchanger of your inward purity. He will be purifying you all the time and lifting you higher, and you will know you are not of this world (John 15:19).

Our Heavenly Dwelling

You are not of this world. If you want to stay in the world, you cannot go on with God. If you are not of this world, your position in the world in your banking affairs and everything else will have the least effect on you. Yet you will know that everything will work for your good if you climb the ladder of faith with God. God will keep the world in perfect order and give you success in the end.

But God cannot work for you; you are so involved in the world that He cannot get your attention. How can someone get into this divine order when he is torn between these two things: God and the world? He cannot let himself go and let God take him.

Let us read the passage from 2 Corinthians again, starting from the seventeenth verse:

For our light affliction, which is but for a moment, worketh for us a far more exceeding and eternal weight of glory; while we look not at the things which are seen, but at the things which are not seen: for the things which are seen are temporal; but the things which are not seen are eternal. For we know that if our earthly house of this tabernacle were dissolved, we have a building of God, an house not made with hands, eternal in the heavens.

(2 Cor. 4:17–5:1 KJV)

I maintain that, by the grace of God, we are so rich, we are so abounding, we have such a treasure-house, we have such a storehouse of God, we have such an unlimited faith to share in all that God has, for it is ours. We are the cream of the earth; we are the precious fruit of the earth.

God has told us that all things will work together for our good (Rom. 8:28). God has said that we will be the *"children of the Highest"* (Luke 6:35 KJV) and that we will be the *"salt of the earth"* (Matt. 5:13). God has declared all that in His Word, and you will never reach those beatitudes if you are holding on to the lower things of this world; they will keep you down.

How am I to have all the treasures of heaven and all the treasures of God? Not by getting my eyes on the things that are seen, for they will fade away. I must get my eyes on the things that are not seen, for they will remain as long as God reigns.

Where are we? Are our eyes on the earth? You once had your eyes on the earth. All your members were in the earth, working out the plan of the earth. But now a change is taking place. I read in the Scriptures: *"That you may be married to another; to Him who was raised from the dead, that we should bear fruit to God"* (Rom. 7:4).

You are joined to Another; you belong to Another. You have a new life; you have a new place. God has changed you. Is it a living fact? If it is only a word, it will end there. But if it is a spiritual fact, and you reign in it, you will go away from this meeting and say, "Thank God, I never knew I was so rich!" How to loose and how to bind in the Spirit—these are great ideals.

DISSOLVED AND MADE LIKE CHRIST

I want you to see that there are two aspects to this: there is a swallowing up (2 Cor. 5:4) and a dissolving (v. 1 KJV). I like the thought of dissolving.

Will that dissolving take place while we are still living on earth? We will not want it to be any other way. When will the clothing upon take place so that we may not be naked (v. 3)? It will take place while we live on earth. People believe that these conditions are not attainable while we live, but all these are spiritual blessings that *are* attainable while we live. These beatitudes dovetail so perfectly with those in the fifth chapter of Matthew's gospel. We will have to wake up and see that there are so many things in that fifth chapter of Matthew's gospel that are as practical as can be. Then God will be able to trust us with them along these lines.

I want us to grasp this idea of dissolving: *"For we know that if our earthly house of this tabernacle were dissolved, we have a building of God, an house not made with hands, eternal in the heavens"* (2 Cor. 5:1 KJV).

That is a perfect condition of a heavenly atmosphere and dwelling place. Let me take you there today. If I live on the earth, I fail everything. If I continue on the earth, everything I do will be mortal and will die. If I live in the heavenly realms, in the heavenly places, everything I touch will become spiritual, vital, purified, and eternal.

I must comprehend today by the faith of God how everything can be dissolved. I will explain it to you first in its heavenly connotation because you will understand it better that way. I will talk about it in regard to the Rapture, for that is what everyone focuses on in this chapter. They say, "Some day we will leave the earth, and everything will be dissolved, and we will be clothed with new bodies for heavenly conditions."

But let me now explain a different way of looking at it. What is the good of having a white raiment to cover your nakedness so that it may not be seen in heaven? You know very well that isn't a heavenly condition. There will be no flesh in heaven. No nakedness will be seen in heaven. Then what does it really mean? It means that the power of God can so dwell in us that it can burn up everything that is not spiritual and dissolve it to the perfection of beauty and holiness that Jesus has. He walked on this earth, and when Satan came, he could find nothing in Him. (See John 14:30.) Jesus was perfectly dissolved in regard to everything in His human nature, and He lived in the Spirit over everything else. As He is, so we have to be. (See 1 John 4:17.)

We shouldn't be troubled in the flesh. Was Jesus troubled in the flesh? Didn't He go forth with perfect victory? It is impossible for any avenue of flesh, or anything that you touch in your natural body, to be helpful. Even your eyes have to be sanctified by the power of God so that they strike fire every time you look at a sinner, and the sinner will be changed.

We will be clothed with a robe of righteousness in God so that wherever we walk, there will be a whiteness of effectiveness that will bring people to a place of conviction of sin. You say, "There are so many things in my house that would have to be thrown out the window if Jesus came to my home." I pray that we could understand that He is already in the house all the time. Everything ought to go out the window that couldn't stand His eyes on it. Every impression of our hearts that would bring trouble if He looked at us ought to go forever.

You ask, "What are we to do?" It is in the message I am preaching; we are to be *"swallowed up by life"* (2 Cor. 5:4). The great I AM in perfect holiness—is He only an example? By the grace of God, He isn't just the example, but He clothes us with His own nature.

It is impossible for us to subdue kingdoms (see Hebrews 11:33), impossible for the greater works to be accomplished (see John 14:12), impossible for the Son of God to be making sons on earth except as we stand exactly in His place. It is lovely, and I must win Him. There isn't a place in Scripture that God spoke about that He doesn't have for us and which He won't take us into, beloved.

Interpretation of Tongues

It is a whole burnt offering. It is a perfect sacrifice. It is a place where we are perfectly justified, where we have been "partakers of His divine nature," and become personated with His holiness, where we still are there, and He is still in the place of working out His great purpose in us, which is the work of God. "For it is God who works in you to will and to do" these things when we are still and dissolved and put to death, where only the life of Christ is being manifested.

And that is the interpretation of the Spirit. It is both a lofty look and a lowly place.

Understand what "a whole burnt offering" means: a place of ashes, a place of helplessness, a place of wholehearted surrender where you do not refer to yourself. You have no justification of your own in regard to anything. You are prepared to be slandered, to be despised by everybody. You are of no importance to anybody but God. But because of His personality in you, He reserves you for Himself because you are godly, and He sets you on high because you have known His name (Ps. 91:14). He causes you to be the fruit of His loins and to bring forth His glory so that you will not in any way rest in yourself or have any confidence in yourself. Your confidence will be in God. Ah, it is lovely.

"The Lord is the Spirit; and where the Spirit of the Lord is, there is liberty (2 Cor. 3:17).

Interpretation of Tongues
And in the depths of the heart there comes forth to us this morning this truth: "Set your house in order." See to it that you do not allow anything that could be there that He could see that He could be displeased with. Your house is your body; your body is the temple of the Spirit.

See to it that you obey that message.

I wonder how much we know about groaning to be delivered? (See Acts 7:34.) I think I can get an illustration of it by turning to the book of Nehemiah. But before we read a passage from there, please understand that to the Jews, Jerusalem was everything. Jerusalem to the Jews is a great deal now, but it is nothing more to us than any other city. Why? Theirs is an earthly type, but ours is a heavenly one. Our Jerusalem is the glory.

Now, Nehemiah said that one day a report was brought to him:

Our Heavenly Dwelling

Hanani one of my brethren came with men from Judah; and I asked them concerning the Jews who had escaped, who had survived the captivity, and concerning Jerusalem. And they said to me, "The survivors who are left from the captivity in the province are there in great distress and reproach. The wall of Jerusalem is also broken down, and its gates are burned with fire." So it was, when I heard these words, that I sat down and wept, and mourned for many days; I was fasting and praying before the God of heaven. (Neh. 1:2–4)

Nehemiah mourned, fasted, and prayed until his humility and yieldedness before God brought the same thing that God's Word brings to us: it dissolved him. It brought everything of his old nature into a dissolved place where he went right through into the presence of God.

Now Nehemiah was the cupbearer for the Persian king Artaxerxes. The moment the king saw Nehemiah's sad expression, he asked, "What is the matter with you, Nehemiah? I have never seen your countenance changed like this." (See Nehemiah 2:1–2.) Nehemiah was so near almightiness before the king that he could pray and move the heavens and move the king and move the world until Jerusalem was restored.

He mourned. When we reach a place where the Spirit takes us to see our weaknesses, our depravity, our failings; when we mourn before God; we will be dissolved, and in the dissolving, we will be clothed with our house from heaven. We will walk in white; we will be robed with a new robe, and this *"mortality [will] be swallowed up by life"* (2 Cor. 5:4).

Beloved, Christ can bring every one of us, if we will, into a wholehearted dependency where God will never fail us but we will reign in life. We will travail and bring forth fruit; for Zion, when she travails, will make the house of hell shake.

Will we reach this place? Our blessed Lord reached it. Every night He went alone and reached ideals and walked the world in white. He was clothed with the Holy Spirit from heaven.

Daniel entered into the same negotiations with heaven through the same inward aspiration. He groaned and travailed until for three weeks he shook the heavens and moved Gabriel to come. Gabriel passed through all the regions of the damned to bring the message to him.

There was something so beautiful about the whole thing that even Daniel, in his most holy, beautiful state, became as corruption before the presence of Gabriel. And Gabriel strengthened Daniel by his right hand and lifted him up and gave him the visions of the world's history that are to be fulfilled. (See Daniel 9–12.)

Interpretation of Tongues
The lamentable condition where God travails through the soul, touches by the Almighty the man of God like Gabriel, touches the human flesh and changes it and makes it bring forth and "blossom even like the rose"; out of death into life, the powers of God will be.

You cannot get into life except through death, and you cannot get into death except by life. The only way to go into fullness with God is for the life of

Christ to swallow up the natural life. For the natural life to be swallowed up, there must be nothing there but helplessness until the life of Christ strengthens the natural life. Yet instead of the natural life being strengthened, the spiritual life comes forth with abounding conditions.

KNOW NO MAN ACCORDING TO THE FLESH

Much has been given this morning in the Spirit that has never been given by me before, and I know that God has brought this message through a travail; it has come this morning for us. It will mean a lot more to us if we don't let these things slip. Let us grasp something from the sixteenth verse: *"Therefore, from now on, we regard no one according to the flesh. Even though we have known Christ according to the flesh, yet now we know Him thus no longer"* (2 Cor. 5:16).

To no longer know any man according to the flesh is a great thing. Beloved, we will no longer know any man along natural lines. From this moment, we will know everything only on a spiritual basis. Conversation must be spiritual. We can get distracted after we have had a really good meal; instead of no longer knowing any man according to the flesh, so that everything is in spiritual fellowship and union, we lower the standard by talking about natural things.

If you ride with me in a train compartment, you will have to pray or testify. If you don't, you will hear a whole lot of talk that will lower the anointing, bring you into a kind of bondage, and make you feel you wish you were out of the compartment. But if you break in and have a prayer meeting, you will turn the whole thing around. Go in and pray until you know everybody has been touched by it.

If you go out to dinner with anybody today, don't get sidetracked by listening to a long story about the state of their businesses. You must know only one Man now, and that is Christ, and He hasn't any businesses. Yet He is Lord over all businesses. Live in the Spirit, and all things will work together for good to you (Rom. 8:28). If you live for your businesses, you will not know the mind of the Spirit. However, if you live in the heavenly places, you will cause your businesses and all things to come out of their difficulties, for God will fight for you.

"We regard no one according to the flesh" (2 Cor. 5:16). I won't enter into anything that is lower than spiritual fidelity. When I am preaching spiritually anointing thoughts, I must see that I lift my people into a place where I know the Spirit is leading me to know Jesus.

Suppose you know Jesus. What do you say? That He lost out? No, He didn't. But a great deal was put upon Him by the people who said,

> *Is this not the carpenter's son? Is not His mother called Mary? And His brothers James, Joses, Simon, and Judas? And His sisters, are they not all with us? Where then did this Man get all these things?* (Matt. 13:55–56)

They said, "He is only an ordinary man. He was born the same way we all were. You see Him. So what is He?"

You will never get anything that way. He wasn't an ordinary man if He was born out of the "loins of Abraham." Two sons were born to Abraham: Isaac and Ishmael. One was the son of promise, the other wasn't. But Isaac, the son of promise, got the blessings. Isaac was a type of Christ. You can never enter into God's conditions in any way but the spiritual way.

For a time, a cloud overshadowed Jesus because of His ancestry. With the Jews, it overshadows Him today because the veil is over their eyes; but the veil will be lifted. (See 2 Corinthians 3:14–16.) With the Gentiles, the veil is already lifted.

We see Him as the Incarnation, as the Holy One of God, as the Son of God, as the *"only begotten of the Father, full of grace and truth"* (John 1:14). We see Him as the Burden-Bearer, as our Sanctifier, as our Cleanser, as our Baptizer. Know no man according to the flesh, but see Him! As we behold Him in all His glory, we will rise; we cannot help but rise in the power of God.

Know no man according to the flesh. You will draw people if you refuse to be contaminated by the world. People want holiness. People want righteousness. People want purity. People have an inward longing to be clothed with the Spirit.

May the Lord lead you to the supply of every need, far more than you can *"ask or think"* (Eph. 3:20). May the Lord bless you as you are led to dedicate yourself afresh to God this very day. Amen.

8

Clothed with the Spirit

od has a plan for us in this life of the Spirit, this abundant life. Jesus came so that we might have life (John 10:10). Satan comes to steal and kill and destroy (v. 10), but God has abundance for us—full measure, pressed down, shaken together, overflowing, abundant measure (Luke 6:38). This abundance is God filling us with His own personality and presence, making us salt and light and giving us a revelation of Himself. It is God with us in all circumstances, afflictions, persecutions, and trials, girding us with truth. Christ the Initiative, the Triune God, is in control, and our every thought, word, and action must be in line with Him, with no weakness or failure. Our God is a God of might, light, and revelation, preparing us for heaven. Our lives are *"hidden with Christ in God"* (Col. 3:3). When He who is our life is manifested, we will also *"appear with Him in glory"* (v. 4).

THE GUARANTEE OF THE SPIRIT

For we know that if our earthly house, this tent, is destroyed, we have a building from

> *God, a house not made with hands, eternal in the heavens....For we who are in this tent groan, being burdened, not because we want to be unclothed, but further clothed, that mortality may be swallowed up by life. Now He who has prepared us for this very thing is God, who also has given us the Spirit as a guarantee.* (2 Cor. 5:1, 4–5)

God's Word is a tremendous word, a productive word. It produces what it is—power. It produces Godlikeness. We get to heaven through Christ, the Word of God; we have peace through the blood of His cross. Redemption is ours through the knowledge of the Word. I am saved because God's Word says so: *"If you confess with your mouth the Lord Jesus and believe in your heart that God has raised Him from the dead, you will be saved"* (Rom. 10:9).

If I am baptized with the Holy Spirit, it is because Jesus said, *"You shall receive power when the Holy Spirit has come upon you"* (Acts 1:8). We must all have one thought—to be filled with the Holy Spirit, to be filled with God.

Interpretation of Tongues

God has sent His Word to free us from the "law of sin and death." Except we die, we cannot live; except we cease to be, God cannot be.

The Holy Spirit has a royal plan, a heavenly plan. He came to unveil the King, to show the character of God, to unveil the precious blood of Jesus. Because I have the Holy Spirit within me, I see Jesus clothed for humanity. He was moved by the Spirit, led by the Spirit. We read of some who heard the Word of God but did not benefit from it because faith was lacking in them (Heb. 4:2). We must have a living faith in God's Word, a faith that is quickened by the Spirit.

A man may be saved and still be carnally minded. When many people hear about the baptism of the Holy Spirit, their carnal minds at once arise against the Holy Spirit. *"The carnal mind...is not subject to the law of God, nor indeed can be"* (Rom. 8:7). One time, Jesus' disciples wanted to call down fire from heaven as a punishment against a Samaritan village for not welcoming Him. But Jesus said to them, *"You do not know what manner of spirit you are of"* (Luke 9:55).

> *For we who are in this tent groan, being burdened, not because we want to be unclothed, but further clothed, that mortality may be swallowed up by life. Now He who has prepared us for this very thing is God, who also has given us the Spirit as a guarantee.*
>
> *(2 Cor. 5:4–5)*

When we are clothed with the Spirit, our human depravity is covered and everything that is contrary to the mind of God is destroyed. God must have people for Himself who are being clothed with a heavenly habitation, perfectly prepared by the Holy Spirit for the Day of the Lord. *"For in this we groan, earnestly desiring to be clothed with our habitation which is from heaven"* (v. 2).

Was Paul speaking here only about the coming of the Lord? No. Yet this condition of preparedness on earth is related to our heavenly state. The Holy Spirit is coming to take out of the world a church that is a perfect bride. He must find in us perfect yieldedness, with every desire subjected to Him. He has come to reveal Christ in us so that the glorious flow of the life of God may flow out of us, bringing rivers of living water to the thirsty land.

"If Christ is in you, the body is dead because of sin, but the Spirit is life because of righteousness" (Rom. 8:10).

THE PLAN OF THE SPIRIT

Interpretation of Tongues
This is what God has declared: freedom from the law. "If we love the world, the love of the Father is not in us."

"For all that is in the world; the lust of the flesh, the lust of the eyes, and the pride of life; is not of the Father but is of the world" (1 John 2:16).

The Spirit has to breathe into us a new occupancy, a new order. He came to give the vision of a life in which Jesus is perfected in us.

> [God] *has saved us and called us with a holy calling, not according to our works, but according to His own purpose and grace which was given to us in Christ Jesus before time began, but has now been revealed by the appearing of our Savior Jesus Christ, who has abolished death and brought life and immortality to light through the gospel.*
>
> *(2 Tim. 1:9–10)*

Clothed with the Spirit

We are saved, called with a holy calling—called to be saints, holy, pure, Godlike, sons with power. It has been a long time now since the debt of sin was settled, our redemption was secured, and death was abolished. Mortality is a hindrance, but death no longer has power. Sin no longer has dominion. You reign in Christ; you appropriate His finished work. Don't groan and travail for a week if you are in need; *"only believe"* (Mark 5:36). Don't fight to get some special thing; *"only believe."* It is according to your faith that you will receive (Matt. 9:29). God blesses you with faith. *"Have faith in God"* (Mark 11:22). If you are free in God, believe, and it will come to pass.

"If then you were raised with Christ, seek those things which are above, where Christ is, sitting at the right hand of God" (Col. 3:1). Stir yourselves up, beloved! Where are you? I have been planted with Christ in the likeness of His death, and I am risen with Christ (Rom. 6:5 KJV). It was a beautiful planting. I am seated with Him in heavenly places (Eph. 2:6). God credits me with righteousness through faith in Christ (Rom. 4:5), and I believe Him. Why should I doubt?

Interpretation of Tongues
Why do you doubt? Faith reigns. God makes it possible. How many receive the Holy Spirit, and Satan gets a doubt in? Don't doubt; believe. There is power and strength in Him; who will dare to believe God?

Leave Doubting Street; live on Faith-Victory Street. Jesus sent the seventy out, and they came back in victory. (See Luke 10:1–18.) It takes God to make it real. Dare to believe until there is not a sick person, until there is no sickness, until everything that is not of God is withered, and the life of Jesus is implanted within.

9

Filled with God

et us begin by reading the second chapter of Hebrews. This passage, like every other Scripture, is very important for us. At first read, we could scarcely pick any special Scripture out of this passage, for it is all so full of truth. It means so much to us.

Therefore we must give the more earnest heed to the things we have heard, lest we drift away. For if the word spoken through angels proved steadfast, and every transgression and disobedience received a just reward, how shall we escape if we neglect so great a salvation, which at the first began to be spoken by the Lord, and was confirmed to us by those who heard Him, God also bearing witness both with signs and wonders, with various miracles, and gifts of the Holy Spirit, according to His own will? For He has not put the world to come, of which we speak, in subjection to angels. But one testified in a certain place, saying: "What is man that You are mindful of him, or the son of man

*that You take care of him? You have made him
a little lower than the angels; You have
crowned him with glory and honor, and set
him over the works of Your hands. You have
put all things in subjection under his feet."
For in that He put all in subjection under him,
He left nothing that is not put under him. But
now we do not yet see all things put under
him. But we see Jesus, who was made a little
lower than the angels, for the suffering of death
crowned with glory and honor, that He, by the
grace of God, might taste death for everyone.
For it was fitting for Him, for whom are all
things and by whom are all things, in bringing
many sons to glory, to make the captain of
their salvation perfect through sufferings. For
both He who sanctifies and those who are being sanctified are all of one, for which reason
He is not ashamed to call them brethren, saying: "I will declare Your name to My brethren;
in the midst of the assembly I will sing praise
to You." And again: "I will put My trust in
Him." And again: "Here am I and the children whom God has given Me." Inasmuch
then as the children have partaken of flesh and
blood, He Himself likewise shared in the same,
that through death He might destroy him who
had the power of death, that is, the devil, and
release those who through fear of death were
all their lifetime subject to bondage. For indeed He does not give aid to angels, but He
does give aid to the seed of Abraham. Therefore, in all things He had to be made like His
brethren, that He might be a merciful and
faithful High Priest in things pertaining to*

Filled with God

God, to make propitiation for the sins of the people. For in that He Himself has suffered, being tempted, He is able to aid those who are tempted. *(Heb. 2:1–18)*

We must understand that God, in these times, wants to bring us into perfect life so that we never, under any circumstances, need to go outside of His Word for anything.

Some people come to God with only a very small idea of His fullness, and a lot of people are satisfied with just a thimbleful. You can just imagine God saying, "Oh, if they only knew how much they could receive!" Other people come with a larger vessel, and they go away satisfied. But you can feel how much God is longing for us to have such a desire for more, such a longing as only He Himself can satisfy.

ONLY GOD CAN SATISFY

I suppose the women here would have a good idea of what I mean from the illustration of a screaming child being taken around from one person to another but never satisfied until he gets to the arms of his mother. You will find that there is no peace, no help, no source of strength, no power, no life, nothing that can satisfy the cry of the child of God but the Word of God. God has a special way of satisfying the cry of His children. He is waiting to open to us the windows of heaven until He has so moved in the depths of our hearts that everything unlike Himself has been destroyed. No one in this place needs to go away dry. God wants you to be filled. My brother, my sister, God wants you today to be like a watered garden, filled with the fragrance of His own heavenly joy, until you know at last that you have touched immensity. The Son of God came for no other purpose than to lift and lift and mold and fashion and remold us until we become conformed to His own mind.

I know that the dry ground can have floods, and may God save me from ever wanting anything less than a flood. I will not stoop for small things when I have such a big God. Through the blood of Christ's atonement, we may have riches and riches. We need the warming atmosphere of the Spirit's power to bring us closer and closer until nothing but God can satisfy, and then we may have some idea of what God has left over after we have taken all that we can. It is just like a sparrow taking a drink of the ocean and then looking around and saying, "What a vast ocean! What a lot more I could have taken if I had only had room."

You may sometimes have things you can use, and not know it. Don't you know that you can be dying of thirst right in the middle of a river of plenty? There was once a vessel in the mouth of the Amazon river. Those on board thought they were still in the ocean, and they were dying of thirst; some of them had nearly been driven mad. They saw a ship and asked if they could have some water, for some of them were dying of thirst. Those on the other ship replied, "Dip your bucket right over; you are in the mouth of the river." There are many people today who are in the midst of a great river of life but are dying of thirst because they do not dip down and take it. Dear friend, you may have the Word, but you need an awakened spirit. The Word is not alive until it is moved upon by the Spirit of God, and in the right sense it becomes Spirit and life (John 6:63) when it is touched by His hand alone.

Beloved, there is a stream that makes glad the city of God (Ps. 46:4). There is a stream of life that makes everything move. There is a touch of divine life and likeness through the Word of God that comes from nowhere else. There is a death that has no life in it, and there is a death-likeness with Christ that is full of life.

Beloved, there is no such thing as an end to God's beginnings. But we must be in Him; we must know Him. The Holy Spirit is not a touch or a breath. He is the Almighty God. He is a person. He is the Holy One dwelling in the temple *"not made with hands"* (2 Cor. 5:1). Beloved, He touches, and it is done. He is the same God over all who is rich unto all who call upon Him (Rom. 10:12). Pentecost is the last thing that God has to touch the earth with. The baptism is the last thing; if you do not get this, you are living in a weak and impoverished condition that is no good to yourself or anybody else. May God move us on to a place where there is no measure to this fullness that He wants to give us. God exalted Jesus and gave Him a name above every name (Phil. 2:9). Notice that everything has been put under Him (Eph. 1:22).

In the last eight years or so, I have seen thousands and thousands of people healed by the power of God. Last year in Sweden, the last five months of the year, we saw over seven thousand people saved by the power of God. The tide is rolling in; let us see to it today that we get right out into the tide, for it will bear us. The heart of God's love is the center of all things. Get your eyes off yourself; lift them up high and see the Lord, *"for in the LORD...is everlasting strength"* (Isa. 26:4 KJV).

DOCTOR JESUS

If you went to see a doctor, the more you told him, the more he would know. But when you come to Doctor Jesus, He knows everything from the beginning, and He never gives you the wrong medicine. I went to see a doctor today, and someone in the doctor's office said, "Here is a person who has been poisoned through and through by another doctor giving him the wrong medicine." But Jesus sends His healing power and brings His restoring grace, and so there is nothing to fear. The only thing that is wrong is your wrong conception of the mightiness of His redemption.

He was wounded so that He might be touched with a feeling of your infirmities. He took your flesh and laid it upon the cross so that *"he might destroy him that had the power of death, that is, the devil; and deliver them who through fear of death were all their lifetime subject to bondage"* (Heb. 2:14–15 KJV).

You will find that almost all the ailments that you are heir to are satanically caused, and they must be dealt with as satanic; they must be cast out. Do not listen to what Satan says to you, for the Devil has been a liar from the beginning (John 8:44). If people would only listen to the truth of God, they would find out that they are over the Devil, over all satanic forces; they would realize that every evil spirit is subject to them. They would find out that they are always in the place of triumph, and they would *"reign in life"* (Rom. 5:17) by King Jesus.

Filled with God

Never live in a place that is less than where God has called you to, and He has called you up on high to live with Him. God has designed that everything will be subject to man. Through Christ, He has given you *"power...over all the power of the enemy"* (Luke 10:19 KJV). He has worked out your eternal redemption.

RECEIVE EVERYTHING YOU CAME FOR

When I had finished a meeting one day in Switzerland, and when I and those with me had ministered to all the sick, we went out to see some people. Two boys came to us and said that there was a blind man present at the meeting that afternoon who had heard all the words of the preacher. He said he was surprised that he had not been prayed for. They went on to say that this blind man had heard so much that he would not leave that place until he could see. I said, "This is positively unique. God will do something today for that man."

We went back to the place. This blind man said he had never seen before; he had been born blind, but because of the word he had heard preached in the afternoon, he was not going home until he could see. If I ever have joy, it is when I have a lot of people who will not be satisfied until they get all that they have come for. With great joy, I anointed him that day and laid my hands on his eyes, and then immediately God opened his eyes. The man acted very strangely. There were some electric lights in the building; first he counted them and then he counted us. Oh, the ecstatic pleasure that man experienced every moment because he had gained his sight! It made us all feel like weeping and dancing and shouting. Then he pulled out his watch and said that for years he had been feeling the raised figures on the watch in order to tell the time, but now he could look at it and tell us the time. Then, looking as if he had been awakened from some deep sleep or some long, strange dream, he realized that he had never seen the faces of his father and mother, and he went to the door and rushed out. That night, he was the first one in the meeting. All the people knew him as the blind man, and I had to give him a long time to talk about his new sight.

Beloved, I wonder how much you want to take away today. You could not carry it if it were an actual substance. But there is something about the grace and the power and the blessings of God that can be carried, no matter how big they are. Oh, what a Savior! What a place we are in, by grace, that He may come in to commune with us!

He is willing to say to every heart, *"Peace, be still!"* (Mark 4:39), and to every weak body, "Be strong."

Are you going halfway, or are you going right to the end? Do not be deceived today by Satan, but believe God.

10

The Pentecostal Power

ur Scripture text is from the nineteenth chapter of Acts. This passage has many things in it that indicate to us that there was something more marvelous than human power that was manifested in Ephesus:

And it happened, while Apollos was at Corinth, that Paul, having passed through the upper regions, came to Ephesus. And finding some disciples he said to them, "Did you receive the Holy Spirit when you believed?" So they said to him, "We have not so much as heard whether there is a Holy Spirit." And he said to them, "Into what then were you baptized?" So they said, "Into John's baptism." Then Paul said, "John indeed baptized with a baptism of repentance, saying to the people that they should believe on Him who would come after him, that is, on Christ Jesus." When they heard this, they were baptized in the name of the Lord Jesus. And when Paul had laid hands on them, the Holy Spirit came upon them, and they spoke with tongues and prophesied. Now the men were about twelve in

all. And he went into the synagogue and spoke boldly for three months, reasoning and persuading concerning the things of the kingdom of God. But when some were hardened and did not believe, but spoke evil of the Way before the multitude, he departed from them and withdrew the disciples, reasoning daily in the school of Tyrannus. And this continued for two years, so that all who dwelt in Asia heard the word of the Lord Jesus, both Jews and Greeks. Now God worked unusual miracles by the hands of Paul, so that even handkerchiefs or aprons were brought from his body to the sick, and the diseases left them and the evil spirits went out of them. Then some of the itinerant Jewish exorcists took it upon themselves to call the name of the Lord Jesus over those who had evil spirits, saying, "We exorcise you by the Jesus whom Paul preaches." Also there were seven sons of Sceva, a Jewish chief priest, who did so. And the evil spirit answered and said, "Jesus I know, and Paul I know; but who are you?" Then the man in whom the evil spirit was leaped on them, overpowered them, and prevailed against them, so that they fled out of that house naked and wounded. This became known both to all Jews and Greeks dwelling in Ephesus; and fear fell on them all, and the name of the Lord Jesus was magnified. And many who had believed came confessing and telling their deeds. Also, many of those who had practiced magic brought their books together and burned them in the sight of all. And they counted up the value of them, and it totaled fifty thousand pieces of silver. So

The Pentecostal Power

the word of the Lord grew mightily and pre-
vailed. (Acts 19:1–20)

This is a wonderful Scripture passage. When I think about Pentecost, I am astonished from day to day because of its mightiness, its wonderfulness, and how the glory overshadows it. I think sometimes about these things, and they make me feel that we have only just touched the surface of it. Truly it is so, but we must thank God that we have touched it. We must not give in because we have only touched the surface. Whatever God has done in the past, His name is still the same. When hearts are burdened and they come face to face with the need of the day, they look into God's Word, and it brings in a propeller of power or an anointing that makes them know that He has truly visited.

It was a wonderful day when Jesus left the glory to come to earth. I can imagine God the Father and all the angels and all heaven so wonderfully stirred that day when the angels were sent to tell the wonderful story of "peace on earth and good will to men." (See Luke 2:14.) It was a glorious day when they beheld the Babe for the first time and God was looking on. I suppose it would take a big book to contain all that happened after that day up until Jesus was thirty years old. Everything in His life was working up to a great climax. The mother of Jesus hid many of these things in her heart. (See Luke 2:19.)

I know that Pentecost in my life is working up to a climax; it is not all accomplished in a day. There are many waters and all kinds of experiences that we go through before we get to the real summit of everything. The power of God is here to prevail. God is with us.

Now, when Jesus was thirty years old, the time came when it was made manifest at the Jordan River that He was the Son of God. Oh, how beautifully it was made known! It had to be made known first to one who was full of the vision of God. The vision comes to those who are full. Did it ever strike you that we cannot be too full for a vision, that we cannot have too much of God? When a person is full of God, then the visions begin. When God has you in His own plan, what a change; how things operate! You wonder; you see things in a new light. God is being greatly glorified as you yield from day to day. The Spirit seems to lay hold of you and bring you further along. Yes, it is a pressing on, and then He gives us touches of His wonderful power, manifestations of the glory of these things and indications of greater things to follow. These days that we are living in now speak of even better days. How wonderful!

Where would we be today if we had stopped short, if we had not fulfilled the vision that God gave us? I am thinking about the time when Christ sent the Spirit. Saul, who later became the apostle Paul, did not know much about the Spirit. His heart was stirred against the followers of Jesus, his eyes were blinded to the truth, and he was going to put the newborn church to an end in a short time; but Jesus was looking on. We can scarcely understand the whole process—only as God seems to show us—when He gets us into His plan and works with us little by little.

We are all amazed that we are among the "tongues people." It is altogether out of order according to the natural. Some of us would never have been in this Pentecostal movement if we had not been drawn, but God has a wonderful way of drawing us. Paul never intended to be among the disciples; he never intended to have anything to do with this Man called Jesus. But God was working. In the same way, God has been working with us and has brought us to this place. It is marvelous! Oh, the vision of God, the wonderful manifestation that God has for Israel!

I have one purpose in my heart, and it is surely God's plan for me: I want you to see that Jesus Christ is the greatest manifestation in all the world and that His power is unequaled, but that there is only one way to minister it. I want you to notice that in the Scripture passage from Acts 19 that we just looked at, some of the people in Ephesus, after they had seen Paul working wonders by the power of Christ, began to act along natural lines. If I want to do anything for God, I see that it is necessary for me to get the knowledge of God. I cannot work on my own; I must get the vision of God. It must be a divine revelation of the Son of God. It must be that.

I can see as clearly as anything that Saul, in his mad pursuit, had to be stopped along the way. After he was stopped and had the vision from heaven and the light from heaven, he instantly realized that he had been working in the wrong way. And as soon as the power of the Holy Spirit fell upon him, he began in the way in which God wanted him to go. And it was wonderful how he had to suffer to come into the way. (See Acts 9:15–16.) A broken spirit, a tried life, and being driven into a corner as if some strange thing had happened (1 Pet. 4:12)—these are surely the ways in which we to get to know the way of God.

POWER IN THE NAME OF JESUS

Paul did not have any power of his own that enabled him to use the name of Jesus as he did. But when he had to go through the privations and the difficulties, and even when all things seemed as if they were shipwrecked, God stood by him and caused him to know that there was Someone with him, supporting him all the time, who was able to carry him through and bring out what his heart was longing for all the time. He seemed to be so unconsciously filled with the Holy Spirit that all that was needed was to bring the aprons and the handkerchiefs to him and then send them forth to heal and deliver. I can imagine these itinerant Jewish exorcists and these seven sons of Sceva in Ephesus looking on and seeing him and saying, "The power seems to be all in the name. Don't you notice that when he sends out the handkerchiefs and the aprons, he says, 'In the name of the Lord Jesus, I command the evil spirit to come out'?"

These people had been looking around and watching, and they thought, "It is only the name; that is all that is needed," and so they said, "We will do the same." They were determined to make this thing work, and they came to a man who was possessed with an evil power. As they entered into the house where he was, they said, "We charge you in the name of Jesus, whom Paul preaches, to come out." The demon said, *"Jesus I know, and Paul I know; but who are you?"* (Acts 19:15). Then the evil power leaped upon them and tore their clothes off their backs, and they went out naked and wounded.

The Pentecostal Power

It is indeed the name of Jesus that brings power over evil spirits, only they did not understand it. Oh, that God would help us to understand the name of Jesus! There is something in that name that attracts the whole world. It is the name, oh, it is still the name, but you must understand that there is the ministry of the name. It is the Holy Spirit who is behind the ministry. The power is in the knowledge of Him; it is in the ministry of the knowledge of Him, and I can understand that it is only that.

I want to speak about the ministry of the knowledge of Him. This is important. May God help us to understand it. I am satisfied with two things. First, I am satisfied that the power is in the knowledge of His blood and of His perfect holiness. I am perfectly cleansed from all sin and made holy in the knowledge of His holiness. Secondly, I am satisfied that as I know Him; and as I know His power, the same power that works in me as I minister only through the knowledge of Him; and as I know the Christ who is manifested by it; such knowledge will be effective to accomplish the very thing that the Word of God says it will: it will have power over all evil. I minister today in the power of the knowledge of Him. Beyond that, there is a certain sense in which I overcome the world according to my faith in Him. I am more than a conqueror (Rom. 8:37) over everything through the knowledge that I have that He is over everything (Eph. 1:22). He has been crowned by the Father to bring everything into subjection (Eph. 1:22).

Shouting won't cast out an evil spirit, but there is an anointing that is gloriously felt within and brings the act of casting out the demon into perfect harmony with the will of God. We cannot help shouting, though shouting won't do it. The power over evil spirits is in the ministry of the knowledge that He is Lord over all demons, over all powers of wickedness.

Interpretation of Tongues
The Holy One who anointed Jesus is so abiding by the Spirit in the one who is clothed upon to use the name until the glory is manifested and the demons flee; they cannot stand the glory of the manifestation of the Spirit that is manifest.

So I am realizing that Paul went about clothed in the Spirit. This was wonderful. Was his body full of power? No! He sent forth handkerchiefs and aprons that had touched him, and when they touched the needy, they were healed and demons were cast out. Was there power in his body? No! There was power in Jesus. Paul ministered through the power of the anointing of the Holy Spirit and through faith in the name of Jesus.

Interpretation of Tongues
The liberty of the Spirit brings the office.

It is an office; it is a position; it is a place of rest, of faith. Sometimes the demon powers are dealt with in very different ways; they are not all dealt with in the same way. But the ministry of the Spirit is administered by the power of the word *Jesus,* and it never fails to accomplish the purpose that the one in charge has wisdom or discernment to see. This is because along with the Spirit of ministry, there comes the revelation of the need of the one who is bound.

The Pentecostal Power

The Spirit ministers the name of Jesus in many ways. I see it continually happening. I see it working, and all the time the Lord is building up a structure of His own power by a living faith in the sovereignty of Jesus' name. If I turn to John's gospel, I get the whole thing practically in a nutshell: *"This is eternal life, that they may know You, the only true God, and Jesus Christ whom You have sent"* (John 17:3). We must have the knowledge and power of God and the knowledge of Jesus Christ, the embodiment of God, in order to be clothed with God.

I see that there are those who have come into line: they have the blessed Christ within and the power of the baptism, which is the revelation of the Christ of God within. This is so evidenced in the person who is baptized in the Spirit, and the Christ is so plainly abiding, that the moment the person is confronted with evil, he is instantly sensitive to the nature of this confrontation, and he is able to deal with it accordingly.

The difference between the sons of Sceva and Paul was this: They said, "It is only the use of the name that is important." How many people only use the name; how many times are people defeated because they think it is just the name; how many people have been brokenhearted because it did not work when they used the name? If I read this into my text, "He who believes will speak in tongues; he who believes will cast out devils; he who believes will lay hands on the sick and they will recover" (see Mark 16:17–18), it seems perfectly easy on the surface of it. But you must understand this: there are volumes to be applied to the word *believe*. To believe is to believe in the need of the majesty of the glory of the power of God. This is all power, and it brings all other powers into subjection.

WHAT DOES IT MEAN TO BELIEVE?

And what is belief? Let me sum it up in a few sentences. To believe is to have the knowledge of Him in whom you believe. It is not to believe in the word *Jesus,* but to believe in the nature of Christ, to believe in the vision of Christ, for all power has been given unto Him, and greater is He who is within you in the revelation of faith than he who is in the world. (See 1 John 4:4.) And so I say to you, do not be discouraged if every demon has not gone out. The very moment you have gone, do not think that is the end of it. What we have to do is to see that if all it takes is using the name of Jesus, those evil powers would have gone out in that name by the sons of Sceva. It is not that. It is the power of the Holy Spirit with the revelation of the deity of our Christ of glory; it is knowing that all power is given unto Him. Through the knowledge of Christ, and through faith in who He is, demons must surrender, demons must go out. I say this reverently: these bodies of ours are so constructed by God that we may be filled with the divine revelation of the Son of God until it is manifest to the devils we confront, and they will have to go. The Master is in; they see the Master. *"Jesus I know, and Paul I know"* (Acts 19:15). The ministry of the Master! How we need to get to know Him until within us we are full of the manifestation of the King over all demons.

Brothers and sisters, my heart is full. The depths of my yearnings are for the Pentecostal people. My cry is that we will not miss the opportunity of the baptism of the Holy Spirit, that Christ may be manifested in our human frames (2 Cor. 4:10) until every power of evil will be subject to the Christ who is manifested in us. The devils know Jesus.

Two important things are before me. First, to master the situation of myself. You are not going to oppose devils if you cannot master yourself, because you will soon find the devils to be bigger than yourself. It is only when you are conquered by Christ that He is enthroned. Then the embodiment of the Spirit gloriously covers your life so that Jesus is glorified to the full. So first it is the losing of ourselves, and then it is the incoming of Another; it is the glorifying of Him that will fulfill all things, and when He gets hold of lives, He can do it. When God gets hold of your life because you have yielded yourself to Him in this way, He will be delighted to allow the Christ to be so manifested in you that it will be no difficulty for the Devil to know who you are.

I am satisfied that the purpose of Pentecost is to reestablish God in human flesh. Do I need to say it again? The power of the Holy Spirit has to come to be enthroned in the human life so that it does not matter where we find ourselves. Christ is manifested in the place where devils are, the place where religious devils are, the place where false religion and unbelief are, the place where formal religion has taken the place of holiness and righteousness. You need to have holiness—the righteousness and Spirit of the Master—so that in every walk of life, everything that is not like our Lord Jesus will have to depart. That is what is needed today.

I ask you in the Holy Spirit to seek the place where He is in power. *"Jesus I know, and Paul I know; but who are you?"* (Acts 19:15). May God stamp this sobering question upon us, for the Devil is not afraid of us. May the Holy Spirit make us terrors of evildoers today, for the Holy Spirit came into us to judge the world of sin, of unbelief, and of righteousness; that is the purpose of the Holy Spirit. (See John 16:7–11.) Then Jesus will know us, and the devils will know us.

11

Christin Us

believe that God wants to bring to our eyes and our ears a living realization of what the Word of God is, what the Lord God means by what He says, and what we may expect if we believe it. I am certain that the Lord wishes to put before us a living fact that will, by our faith, bring into action a principle that is within our own hearts so that Christ can dethrone every power of Satan.

Only this truth revealed to our hearts can make us so much greater than we ever had any idea we could be. I believe there are volumes of truth right in the midst of our own hearts. There is only the need of revelation and of stirring ourselves up to understand the mightiness that God has within us. We may prove what He has accomplished in us if we will only be willing to carry through what He has already accomplished in us.

For God has not accomplished something in us that should lie dormant, but He has brought within us a power, a revelation, a life that is so great that I believe God wants to reveal the greatness of it. Oh, the possibilities of man in the hands of God! There isn't anything you can imagine that is greater than what man may accomplish through Him.

But everything on a natural basis is very limited compared to what God has for us on a spiritual basis. If man can accomplish much in a short time, what may we accomplish if we will believe the revealed Word and take it as truth that God has given us and that He wants to bring out in revelation and force?

Let us read a passage from the eleventh chapter of the Gospel according to Matthew:

Now it came to pass, when Jesus finished commanding His twelve disciples, that He departed from there to teach and to preach in their cities. And when John had heard in prison about the works of Christ, he sent two of his disciples and said to Him, "Are You the Coming One, or do we look for another?" Jesus answered and said to them, "Go and tell John the things which you hear and see: the blind see and the lame walk; the lepers are cleansed and the deaf hear; the dead are raised up and the poor have the gospel preached to them. And blessed is he who is not offended because of Me." As they departed, Jesus began to say to the multitudes concerning John: "What did you go out into the wilderness to see? A reed shaken by the wind? But what did you go out to see? A man clothed in soft garments? Indeed, those who wear soft clothing are in kings' houses. But what did you go out to see? A prophet? Yes, I say to you, and more than a prophet. For this is he of

whom it is written: 'Behold, I send My messenger before Your face, who will prepare Your way before You.' Assuredly, I say to you, among those born of women there has not risen one greater than John the Baptist; but he who is least in the kingdom of heaven is greater than he. And from the days of John the Baptist until now the kingdom of heaven suffers violence, and the violent take it by force."
(Matt. 11:1–12)

In the first place, notice the fact that John the Baptist was the forerunner of Jesus. Within his own short history, John the Baptist had the power of God revealed to him as probably no man in the old dispensation had. He had a wonderful revelation. He had a mighty anointing.

I want you to see how he moved Israel. I want you to see how the power of God rested upon him. I want you to see how he had the vision of Jesus and went forth with power and turned the hearts of Israel to Him. And yet Jesus said about John:

Among those born of women there has not risen one greater than John the Baptist; but he who is least in the kingdom of heaven is greater than he. *(v. 11)*

Then I want you to see how satanic power can work in the mind. I find that Satan came to John when he was in prison. I find that Satan can come to any of us. Unless we are filled, or divinely insulated, with the power of God, we may be defeated by the power of Satan.

But I want to prove that we have a greater power than Satan's—in imagination, in thought, in everything. Satan came to John the Baptist in prison and said to him, "Don't you think you have made a mistake? Here you are in prison. Isn't there something wrong with the whole business? After all, you may be greatly deceived about being a forerunner of the Christ."

I find men who might be giants of faith, who might be leaders of society, who might rise to subdue kingdoms (Heb. 11:33), who might be noble among princes, but they are defeated because they allow the suggestions of Satan to dethrone their better knowledge of the power of God. May God help us.

See what John the Baptist did:

> *And when John had heard in prison about the works of Christ, he sent two of his disciples and said to Him, "Are You the Coming One, or do we look for another?"*   *(Matt. 11:2–3)*

How could Jesus send those men back with a stimulating truth, with a personal, effective power that would stir their hearts to know that they had met Him about whom all the prophets had spoken? What would declare it? How would they know? How could they tell it?

> *Jesus answered and said to them, "Go and tell John the things which you hear and see: the blind see and the lame walk; the lepers are cleansed and the deaf hear; the dead are raised up and the poor have the gospel preached to them.*   *(vv. 4–5)*

And when they saw the miracles and wonders and heard the gracious words He spoke as the power of God rested upon Him, they were ready to believe.

Have miracles and wonders ceased? If they have not ceased, then I must put before you a living fact. I must cause you to understand why they will not cease. Instead of ceasing, they have to continue to occur. It is only by the grace of God that I dare to put these truths before you because of facts that will be proved.

SONS OF GOD WITH POWER

I have a message for those of you who are saved and a message for those of you who are unsaved, but I want you both to hear. There are none so deaf as those who won't hear, and none so blind as those who won't see. But God has given you ears, and He wants you to hear. What should you hear?

And you shall know the truth, and the truth shall make you free.   *(John 8:32)*

Hear what Jesus said:

As they departed, Jesus began to say to the multitudes concerning John: "What did you go out into the wilderness to see? A reed shaken by the wind?"   *(Matt. 11:7)*

Did you ever see a man of God who was like a reed? If you ever did, I would say that he was only an imitator. Has God ever made a man to be a reed or to be like smoking flax? (See Isaiah 42:3.) No. God wants to make men as flames of fire (Ps. 104:4). God wants to make men *"strong in the Lord and in the power of His might"* (Eph. 6:10).

Therefore, beloved, if you will hear the truth of the Gospel, you will see that God has made provision for you to be strong, to be on fire, to be as though you were quickened from the dead, as those who have seen the King, as those who have a resurrection touch. We know we are the sons of God with power as we believe His Word and stand in the truth of His Word (John 1:12).

Interpretation of Tongues

The Spirit of the Lord breathes upon the slain, and upon the dry bones, and upon the things which are not and changes them in the flesh in a moment of time, and makes what is weak strong. And, behold, He is among us tonight to quicken what is dead and make the dead alive.

He is here!

"The dead will hear the voice of the Son of God; and those who hear will live" (John 5:25). Praise the Lord!

JESUS IS OUR LIFE

Let us move on to another thought in the next verse that is very important: *"And from the days of John the Baptist until now the kingdom of heaven suffers violence, and the violent take it by force"* (Matt. 11:12).

This is a message to every believer. Every believer belongs to the kingdom of heaven. Every believer has the life of the Lord in him. And if Jesus,

Christ in Us

"who is our life" (Col. 3:4), were to come, instantly our life would go out to meet His life because we exist and consist of the life of the Son of God. (See verse 4.) *"Your life is hidden with Christ in God"* (v. 3).

If all believers understood this wonderful passage that is in the twenty-second chapter of Luke's gospel, there would be great joy in their hearts:

> Then He said to them, *"With fervent desire I have desired to eat this Passover with you before I suffer; for I say to you, I will no longer eat of it until it is fulfilled in the kingdom of God."* *(Luke 22:15–16)*

Everyone who is in Christ Jesus will be there when He sits down the first time to break bread in the kingdom of heaven. It is not possible for any child of God to remain on earth when Jesus comes. May the Lord help us to believe it.

I know there is a great deal of speculation on the Rapture and on the coming of the Lord. But let me tell you to hope for edification and comfort, for the Scripture by the Holy Spirit won't let me speak on anything except the edification, consolation, and comfort of the Spirit. (See 1 Corinthians 14:3.) Why? Because we are here for the purpose of giving everybody in the meeting comfort.

I don't mean that we are to cover sin up. God won't let us do that. But we must unveil truth. And what is truth? The Word of God is the truth.

> *I am the way, the truth, and the life.*
> *(John 14:6)*

> *You search the Scriptures, for in them you think you have eternal life; and these are they which testify of Me.* *(John 5:39)*

What does the truth say? It says that when Christ appears, all who are His at His coming will be changed *"in a moment, in the twinkling of an eye"* (1 Cor. 15:52). We will be presented at the same moment as all those who have fallen sleep in Him, and we will all go together.

> *We who are alive and remain until the coming of the Lord will by no means precede those who are asleep....And the dead in Christ will rise first. Then we who are alive and remain shall be caught up together with them in the clouds to meet the Lord in the air. And thus we shall always be with the Lord. Therefore comfort one another with these words.*   *(1 Thess. 4:15–18)*

> *For I say to you, I will not drink of the fruit of the vine until the kingdom of God comes.*
>   *(Luke 22:18)*

Two thousand years will soon have passed since the Lord broke bread around the table with His disciples.

I am longing, the saints are longing, for the grand union when millions, billions, trillions will unite with Him in that great fellowship Supper. Praise the Lord! But now, what stimulation, what power must be working every day until that Day appears!

THE KINGDOM OF HEAVEN

Listen to this carefully; this is my point. (No, it is not my point; it is God's revelation to us. I have nothing to do with it. If I ever say "I" or "my," you must look upon it and forgive me. I don't want to be here to speak my own words, my own thoughts. I want the Lord to be glorified in bringing every thought so that we will all be comforted and edified. But this is a strong message for us and a very helpful one, especially for the sick and needy believer.) This is the point: the kingdom of heaven is within us, within every believer (Luke 17:21). The kingdom of heaven is the Christ; it is the Word of God.

The kingdom of heaven must outstrip everything else, even your own lives. It has to be manifested so that you have to realize that even the death of Christ brings forth the life of Christ.

"The kingdom of heaven suffers violence" (Matt. 11:12). How does the kingdom of heaven suffer violence? If you are suffering, if you are needy—if you have paralysis, or weakness of the head, abdomen, or any other part of the body—if you feel distress in any way, it means that the kingdom of heaven is suffering violence at the hands of the Adversary.

Could the kingdom of heaven bring weaknesses or diseases? Could it bring imperfection on the body? Could it bring tuberculosis? Could it bring extreme fevers, cancers, or tumors?

"The kingdom of God is within you" (Luke 17:21). The kingdom of heaven is the life of Jesus; it is the power of the Highest. The kingdom of heaven is pure; it is holy. It has no disease, no imperfection. It is as holy as God is. And Satan with his evil power *"does not come except to steal, and to kill, and to destroy"* (John 10:10) the body.

Every ailment that anyone has is from a satanic source. It is foolish and ridiculous to think that sickness purifies you. There is no purification in disease. I want you to see the wiles of Satan (Eph. 6:11), the power of the Devil. And I want to show you, in the name of Jesus, your power to dethrone the Enemy.

Oh, this blessed Lord! Oh, this lovely Jesus! Oh, this incarnation of the Lamb who was slain!

Beloved, I wouldn't stand on this platform if I didn't know that the whole Bible is true. Jesus said, *"The [Devil] does not come except to steal, and to kill, and to destroy. I have come that they may have life, and that they may have it more abundantly"* (John 10:10).

I want us to see the difference between the abundant life of Jesus and the power of Satan. Then—by the grace of God—to help us in our position, I want to keep before you this thought: *"The kingdom of heaven suffers"* (Matt. 11:12).

It is only fair and reasonable that I put before you the almightiness of God versus the might of Satan. If Satan were almighty, we would all have to quake with fear. But when we know that Satan is subject to the powers of God in everything, we can get this truth right into our hearts and be conquerors over every situation. I want to make everyone in this meeting *"strong in the Lord and in the power of His might"* (Eph. 6:10).

A POWER GREATER THAN THE ENEMY

I want you to have an inward knowledge that there is a power in you that is greater than any other power. And I trust that, by the help of the Spirit, I may bring you into a place of deliverance, a place of holy sanctification where you dare to stand against the *"wiles of the devil"* (Eph. 6:11), drive them back, and cast them out. May the Lord help us!

If I can wake you up! You ask, "Are we not awake?" You may be cognizant of what I am saying.

You may be able to tell when I lift my hand and put it down. Still, you may be asleep concerning the deep things of God. I want God to give you an inward awakening, a revelation of truth within you, an audacity, a flaming indignation against the powers of Satan.

Lot had a righteous indignation—temporarily— but it came too late. He ought to have had it when he went into Sodom, not when he was coming out. But I don't want any one of you to go away dejected because you didn't take a step in the right direction sooner. Always be thankful that you are alive to hear and to change the situation.

It would be a serious thing for us to pay so much to rent this building, only to have you come in and sit for an hour and a half to two hours and then go out just the same as when you came in. I couldn't stand it. It would all be the biggest foolishness possible, and we would all need to be admitted to the insane asylum.

You must gain an inward knowledge that God is Lord over all the power of Satan. When I speak about you waking up, the thought in my heart is this: I don't doubt your sincerity about being saved, about having been justified in Christ. It is not for me to question a man's sincerity regarding his righteousness. And yet, as I preach to you, I feel I have a right to say that there is a deeper sincerity to reach to, there is a greater audacity of faith and fact to attain. There is something that you have to wake up to where you will never allow disease to have you or sin to have you or a weak heart or a pain in your back to have you. You will never allow anything that isn't perfect life to have anything to do with you.

Let me continue now by showing you the weakness of believers. Does God know all about you? Is He acquainted with you altogether? Why not trust Him who knows all about you, instead of telling somebody else who knows only what you have told him.

Again, why should you, under any circumstances, believe that you will be better off by being diseased? When disease is impurity, why should you ever believe that you will be sanctified by having a great deal of sickness?

Some people talk about God being pleased to put disease on His children. "Here is a person I love," says God. "I will break his arm. Then, so that he will love Me more, I will break his leg. And so that he will love Me still more, I will give him a weak heart. And in order to increase that love, I will make him so that he cannot eat anything without having indigestion."

The whole thing won't stand daylight. And yet people are always talking in this way, and they never think to read the Word of God, which says, *"Before I was afflicted I went astray"* (Ps. 119:67). They have never read the following words into their lives:

> *Fools, because of their transgression, and because of their iniquities, were afflicted. Their soul abhorred all manner of food, and they drew near to the gates of death. Then they cried out to the LORD in their trouble, and He saved them out of their distresses.*
>
> *(Ps. 107:17–19)*

Yes, we have that to praise the Lord for. Is it right now to say, "You know, my brother, I have suffered so much in this affliction that it has made me know God better"? Well, now, before you agree, ask God for a lot more affliction so that you will get to know Him still better. If you won't ask for more affliction to make you still purer, I won't believe that the first affliction made you purer, because if it had, you would have more faith in it. It appears that you do not have faith in your afflictions. It is only talk, but talk doesn't count unless it is backed up by fact. However, if people can see that your words are backed up by fact, then they have some grounds for believing in them.

THE KINGDOM SUFFERS VIOLENCE

I have looked through my Bible, and I cannot find where God brings disease and sickness. I know there is glory, and I know it is the power of God that brings the glory. Yet it is the Devil and not God at all who brings sickness and disease. Why does he? I know this: Satan is God's whip, and if you don't obey God, God will stand to one side and Satan will devour you. But God will only allow him to devour so much, as was the case with Job. The Lord told Satan, "You may go only so far, and no further. Don't touch his life." (See Job 2:6.)

"Let God be true but every man a liar" (Rom. 3:4). I am going to take things on their real basis, on the truth as it is revealed to me in the Scriptures: *"The kingdom of heaven suffers violence"* (Matt. 11:12).

Why is Satan allowed to bring sickness? It is because we know better than we act. And if people would do as well as they know, they would have no sickness. If we would be true to our convictions and walk according to the light we have been given, God would verify His presence in the midst of us, and we would know that sickness cannot *"come near* [our] *dwelling; for He shall give His angels charge over you, to keep you in all your ways"* (Ps. 91:10–11).

If there are weak persons here tonight, and they are suffering terribly, I know they are sorry for their sicknesses. But if they would be as sorry for their sins as they are for their sicknesses, they could be healed. If we ever get desperate about having our sins destroyed, they will go. God help us!

Well, if you are whole from top to bottom and are not distracted by any pain in your body, it is easy to shout "Glory!" But if some people shouted "Glory," one side of them would ache. And so it is with those of you who are not free tonight. I want to put you in a place where you will shout "Glory!"

It is true that God keeps me, as it were, unaware that I have a body. I believe that is part of redemption. But I am not going to condemn people who are not there yet. I am here to help them. But I cannot help you out unless I give you Scripture. If I can lay down a basis in the Word of God for what I am saying, I can send you home and know that you will deliver yourselves.

If I could only get you to catch hold of faith, then, by the grace of God, every person here would be delivered. But I find that Satan has tremendous power over certain functions of the body, and I want to deal with that for a moment in order to help you.

When Satan can get to your body, he will, if possible, make the pain or the weakness so distracting that it will affect your mind and always bring your mind down to where the pain is. When that takes place, you do not have the same freedom in your spirit to lift up your heart and shout and praise the Lord, because the distraction of the pain brings the foundational power, which ought to be full of praise to God, down into the body. And through that—concerning everybody who is afflicted—*"the kingdom of heaven suffers violence"* (Matt. 11:12).

Beloved, I mean precisely this: anything that takes me from a position where I am in an attitude of worship, peace, and joy, where I have a consciousness of the presence of God, where there is an inward moving of the powers of God that makes me able to lift myself up and live in the world as though I were not of it (because I am not of it); anything that dethrones me from that attitude is evil, is Satan.

I want to prove how the kingdom of heaven suffers violence. If it is only a finger or a tooth that aches, if it is only a corn on your foot that pinches you or anything in the body that detracts from the highest spiritual attainment, the kingdom of heaven is dethroned to a degree; *"the kingdom of heaven suffers violence"* (Matt. 11:12).

By the Word of God, I am proving to you that the kingdom of heaven is within you. *"Greater is he that is in you"* (1 John 4:4 KJV)—the Son of God, the kingdom of heaven within you—*"than he that is in the world"* (v. 4 KJV)—the power of Satan outside you.

Disease or weakness, or any distraction in you, is a power of violence that can take the kingdom of heaven in you by force. The same spiritual power that will reveal this to you, will relieve you here in this meeting. For instance, I would like to show you a manifestation of a distraction. Is there a person here who is saved by the power of God but who is suffering in his back, in his legs, in his head, or in his shoulders? (A man raises his hand.)

Stand up, young man. Where are you suffering?

"In my leg."

Stand out in the aisle; this is an example for all the people. Are you saved?

"I am."

Do you believe the kingdom of God is within you?

"I do."

I can prove the Scriptures are true. Here the kingdom of heaven in this man is suffering violence because he has a pain in his leg that takes his mind, a hundred times a day, off the highest enthroned position—where he is seated in heavenly places with Christ Jesus (Eph. 2:6)—and onto his leg. I am going to tell this young man that tonight he has to treat this as an enemy, as the power of Satan down in his legs, and that he has to say that he is free in the name of Jesus. He has to say it by the power that is within him, in fact, by the personality and the presence of God, the power against Satan, the name of Jesus. I want you to say, "In the name of Jesus, come out!" Shout! Put your hand upon your leg and say, "In the name of Jesus, I command you to come out!" Go right to the bottom of your leg. Amen! Praise the Lord! Now walk around. Has he come out? Are you free?

"Yes."

Praise God! On the authority of the Word of God, I maintain that *"greater is he that is in you"* (1 John 4:4) than any power of Satan that is around you (v. 4). Suppose five or six people were standing up tonight, and I prayed with the fact in my heart that in me—by the power of Jesus—is a greater power than the power that is binding them. I pray, I believe, and the evil power goes out while I am praying. How much more would be done if you would inwardly claim your rights and deliver yourselves!

I believe the Bible from front to back. But the Bible won't have an atom of power in you if you don't put it into practice in yourself. If, by the power of God, I put in you an audacity, a determination, so that you won't let Satan rest there, you will be free. Praise the Lord!

Why do I take this attitude? Because for every step of my life since my baptism, I have had to pay the price of everything for others. God has to take me through to the place so that I may be able to show the people how to do it. Some people come up to me and say, "I have been waiting for the baptism, and I am having such a struggle. I am having to fight for every inch of it. Isn't it strange?" No. A thousand to one, God is preparing you to help somebody else who is desiring to receive it.

The reason I am so firm about the necessity of getting the baptism in the Holy Spirit, and about the significance of the Spirit's making a manifestation when He comes in, is this: I fought it. I went to a meeting because I had heard people were speaking in tongues there. I forced myself on the attention of those in the meeting almost like a man who was mad. I told the people there, "This meeting of yours is nothing. I have left better conditions at home. I am hungry and thirsty for something."

"What do you want?" they asked.

"I want tongues."

"You want the baptism?" they asked.

"Not I," I said. "I have the baptism. I want tongues."

I could have had a fight with anybody. The whole situation was this: God was training me for something else. The power of God fell upon my body with such ecstasy of joy that I could not satisfy the joy within with my natural tongue; then I found the Spirit speaking through me in other tongues.

What did it mean? I knew that I had had anointings of joy before this, and expressions of the blessed attitude of the Spirit of life, and joy in the Holy Spirit; I had felt it all the way through my life. But when the fullness came with a high tide, with an overflowing life, I knew that was different from anything else. And I knew that was the baptism, but God had to show me.

People ask, "Do all speak with tongues?" Certainly not. But all people may speak as the Spirit gives utterance—as in the Upper Room and at the house of Cornelius and at Ephesus when Jesus' followers were filled with the Holy Spirit.

There is quite a difference between having a gift and speaking as the Spirit gives utterance. If I had been given the gift of tongues when I was filled with the Holy Spirit, then I could have spoken in tongues at any time, because gifts and calling remain (Rom. 11:29). But I couldn't speak in tongues after I was baptized. Why? It was because I had received the Holy Spirit with the evidence of speaking in tongues, but I hadn't received the gift of tongues.

However, I received the Holy Spirit, who is the Giver of all gifts. And nine months afterward, God gave me the gift of tongues so that I could speak in tongues at any time. But do I? God forbid! Why? Because no man ought to use a gift; the Holy Spirit uses the gift.

I will not be able to bring you into the miraculous regarding what I have been telling you, unless I can provoke you. "Why?" you ask. If I could cause every person who has a bad leg to be so provoked at the Devil that they would kick their bad leg off along with the Devil, then I could get somewhere. You say that I exaggerate. Well, I only exaggerate in order to wake you up.

I have a reason for talking like this. People come up to me all the time and say, "I have been prayed for, and I am just the same." It is enough to make you kick them. I don't mean that literally. I would be the last man to kick anybody in this place. God forbid. *"For the weapons of our warfare are not carnal but mighty in God for pulling down strongholds"* (2 Cor. 10:4). But if I can get you enraged against the powers of darkness and the powers of disease, if I can wake you up, you won't go to bed unless you prove that there is a Master in you who is greater than the power that is hanging around you.

Many times I have gone to a house in which an insane person lived and have been shut in with him in order to deliver him. I have gone in determined that he would be delivered. In the middle of the night chiefly, sometimes in the middle of the day, the demon powers would come and bite me and handle me terribly roughly. But I never gave in. It would dethrone a higher principle if I had to give in.

There is a great cloud of witnesses of the satanic powers from hell. We are here on probation to slay the Enemy and destroy the kingdoms of darkness, to move among satanic forces and subdue them in the name of Jesus.

May the God of grace and mercy strengthen us. If the five or six hundred people in this place tonight were—in the will of God—to rise as one man to slay the Enemy, the evil host around us would feel the power. And in the measure that we destroy these evil powers, we make it easier for weak believers. For every time Satan overcomes a saint, it gives him ferocity for another attack; but when he is subdued, he will come to the place where defeat is written against him.

If you know God is within you, and you are suffering in any part of your body, please stand. I would like to take another case to prove my position in order to help all the people here. (A woman stands.) You know you are saved?

"Yes, sir."

Praise God! Do you know this truth from the fourth chapter of the first epistle of John: *"Greater is he that is in you, than he that is in the world"* (v. 4 KJV)? What is the trouble with you?

"I am suffering from neuralgic pains."

Then by the authority of Jesus, where the neuralgia is, you go like this: "I rebuke you in the name of Jesus! I am against you! In the name of Jesus, come out and leave me!" Now, go on.

"I rebuke you in the name of Jesus! I refuse this pain to remain in the name of Jesus."

I believe it is gone. Is it gone?

"It is gone!"

Let me read to you what I have been preaching, because I want to prove that it is the Word of God. It is in the eleventh chapter of Matthew: *"And from the days of John the Baptist until now* [right up to this moment] *the kingdom of heaven suffers violence"* (v. 12). That is, the inward presence of God suffers violence by the power of Satan. *"And the violent take it by force"* (v. 12).

How many people in this meeting are going to try that before going to bed? Glory to God! That is faith.

> I know the Lord, I know the Lord,
> I know the Lord's laid His hand on me.

If anyone were to say to me, "Wigglesworth, I will give you ten thousand dollars," in my estimation it would be as dust compared to the rising faith I have just seen. What I have seen by your uplifted hands along the lines of faith is of more value to me than anything you could count.

In your home, with your wife and children, you will have audacity of determination, along with a righteous indignation, against the power of disease to cast it out. That is worth more to you than anything you could buy.

I have a clear conviction that through the preached Word, there are people who are going to take a new step. By the grace of God, we have seen tonight that we have to keep authority over the body, making the body subject to the higher powers. What about you who are in sickness or who are bound in other ways: don't you long to come into a fullness of God? Aren't you longing to know a Savior who can preserve you in the world over the powers of the Enemy? I pray tonight, in the name of Jesus, that you will yield.

Everyone who has an inward knowledge of an indwelling Christ, lift your right hand. Thank God! Put them down. No one can have a knowledge of an inward Christ without having a longing that there will be an increase of souls saved. The very first principle is that you have a *"first love"* (Rev. 2:4). And if you don't lose that love, it will keep you focused on winning souls all the time.

Those of you who did not put up your hands before, do you dare to put up your hands now and let all those four hundred believers pray for you? While we all appreciate the penitent bench being filled, I know that if you cannot be saved in your seats, you cannot be saved up here. You are not saved by coming forward, although it is a help for you to come forward. But if these four hundred saved people pray for you who have no knowledge of salvation, you can be saved right where you are.

So I am going to give you a real live opportunity to get near God by standing on your feet with these four hundred and sweeping into the kingdom of heaven by faith.

> Jesus paid it all,
>   All to Him I owe;
> Sin had left a crimson stain;
>   He washed it white as snow.

12

Aflame for God

he word that I have for you is Hebrews 1:7: *"And of the angels He says: 'Who makes His angels spirits and His ministers a flame of fire.'"* His ministers are to be flames of fire! It seems to me that no man with a vision, especially a vision by the Spirit's power, can read that wonderful verse without being kindled to such a flame of fire for his Lord that it seems as if it would burn up everything that would interfere with his progress

A flame of fire! It is a perpetual fire; a constant fire; a continual burning; a holy, inward flame; which is exactly what God's Son was in the world. I can see that God has nothing less for us than to be flames! It seems to me that if Pentecost is to rise and be effective, we must have a living faith so that Christ's great might and power can flow through us until our lives become energized, moved, and aflame for God.

The important point of this message is that the Holy Spirit has come to make Jesus King. It seems to me that the seed, the life that was given to us when we believed—which is an eternal seed—has such resurrection power that I see a new creation rising from it with kingly qualities. I see that when we are baptized in the Holy Spirit, it is to crown Jesus King in our lives. Not only is the King to be within us, but also all the glories of His kingly manifestations are to be brought forth in us. Oh, for Him to work in us in this way, melting us, until a new order rises within us so that we are moved with His compassion. I see that we can come into the order of God where the vision becomes so much brighter and where the Lord is manifesting His glory with all His virtues and gifts; all His glory seems to fill the soul who is absolutely dead to himself and alive to God. There is much talk about death, but there is a death that is so deep in God that, out of that death, God brings the splendor of His life and all His glory.

An opportunity to be a flame of fire for God came when I was traveling from Egypt to Italy. What I now tell you truly happened. On the ship and everywhere, God had been with me. A man on the ship suddenly collapsed; his wife was in a terrible state, and everybody else seemed to be, too. Some said that he would die, but oh, to be a flame, to have the living Christ dwelling within you!

We are backslidden if we have to pray for power, if we have to wait until we feel a sense of His presence. The baptism of the Holy Spirit has come upon you: *"You shall receive power when the Holy Spirit has come upon you"* (Acts 1:8). Within you is a greater power than there is in the world (1 John 4:4). Oh, to be awakened out of our unbelief into a place of daring for God on the authority of the blessed Book!

So in the name of Jesus, I rebuked the devil, and to the astonishment of the man's wife and the man himself, he was able to stand. He said, "What is this? It is going all over me. I have never felt anything like this before." From the top of his head to the soles of his feet, the power of God shook him. God has given us authority over the power of the Devil. Oh, that we may live in the place where the glory excels! It would make anyone a flame of fire.

Christ, who is the express image of God (Heb. 1:3), has come to our human weaknesses in order to change them and us into a divine likeness so that, by the power of His might, we may not only overcome but rejoice in the fact that we are more than overcomers. God wants you to be *"more than conquerors"* (Rom. 8:37)! The baptism of the Spirit has come for nothing less than to possess the whole of our lives. It sets up Jesus as King, and nothing can stand in His holy presence when He is made King. Everything will wither before Him. I feel that the reason I come to a meeting like this is to stir you up and help you know that the inheritance of the Spirit is given to every man *"for the profit of all"* (1 Cor. 12:7). Praise the Lord! In the order of the Holy Spirit, we have to *"come short in no gift"* (1 Cor. 1:7).

This same Jesus has come for one purpose: that He might be made so manifest in us that the world will see Him. We must be burning and shining lights to reflect such a holy Jesus. We cannot do it with cold, indifferent experiences, and we never will. My dear wife used to say to our daughter, "Alice, what kind of a meeting have you had?" Alice would say, "Ask Father. He always has a good time!" His servants are to be flames. Jesus is life, and the Holy

Spirit is the breath. He breathes through us the life of the Son of God, and we give it to others, and it gives life everywhere.

You should have been with me in Ceylon! I was having meetings in a Wesleyan chapel. The people there said, "You know, four days are not much to give us." "No," I said, "but it is a good share." They said, "What are we going to do? We are not touching the people here at all." I said, "Can you have a meeting early in the morning, at eight o'clock?" They said they would, so I said, "We will tell all the mothers who want their babies to be healed and all the old people over seventy to come. Then after that, I will hope to give an address to the people to make them ready for the Holy Spirit."

Oh, it would have done you all good to see four hundred mothers there with their babies! It was fine! And then to see one hundred and fifty old black people, with their white hair, coming to be healed. I believe that you need to have something more than smoke to touch people; you need to be a burning light for that. His ministers must be flames of fire. There were thousands gathered outside the chapel to hear the Word of God. There were about three thousand people crying for mercy at the same time. I tell you, it was a sight.

After that, attendance at the meetings rose to such an extent that every night, five to six thousand people gathered there after I had preached in a temperature of 110 degrees. Then I had to minister to these people. But I tell you, a flame of fire can do anything. Things change in the fire. This is Pentecost. But what moved me more than anything else was this (and I say this carefully and with a broken spirit because I would not like to mislead anybody): there were hundreds who tried to touch me because they were so impressed with the power of God that was present. And they testified everywhere that with a touch, they were healed. It was *not* the power of Wigglesworth. It was because they had the same faith that was with those at Jerusalem who believed that Peter's shadow would heal them. (See Acts 5:14–15.)

You can receive something in three minutes that you can carry with you into glory. What do you want? Is anything too hard for God? God can meet you now. God sees inwardly. He knows all about you. Nothing is hidden from Him, and He can satisfy the soul and give you a spring of eternal blessing that will carry you right through.

13

"Glory and Virtue"

want you to see two words that are closely connected: *glory* and *virtue*. They are beautiful words and are full of blessing for us this moment. Let me read the verse in which they are found: *"Through the knowledge of Him who called us by glory and virtue"* (2 Pet. 1:3).

People have a great misunderstanding about glory, though they often use the word. There are three things that ought to take place at the baptism of the Holy Spirit. It was necessary that the movement of the mighty rushing wind was made manifest in the Upper Room and that the disciples were clothed with tongues as of fire. (See Acts 2:1–4.) Also, it was necessary that they received not only the fire but also the rushing wind, the personality of the Spirit in the wind. The manifestation of the glory is in the wind, or breath, of God.

The inward man receives the Holy Spirit instantly with great joy and blessedness. He cannot express it. Then the power of the Spirit, this breath of God, takes of the things of Jesus (see John 16:14–15) and sends forth as a river the utterances of the

Spirit. Again, when the body is filled with joy, sometimes so inexpressible, and the joy is thrown on the canvas of the mind, the canvas of the mind has great power to move the operation of the tongue to bring out the very depths of the inward heart's power, love, and joy to us. By the same process, the Spirit, which is the breath of God, brings forth the manifestation of the glory.

Peter said in 2 Peter 1:16–17,

For we did not follow cunningly devised fables when we made known to you the power and coming of our Lord Jesus Christ, but were eyewitnesses of His majesty. For He received from God the Father honor and glory when such a voice came to Him from the Excellent Glory: "This is My beloved Son, in whom I am well pleased."

Sometimes people wonder why it is that the Holy Spirit is always expressing Himself in words. It cannot be otherwise. You could not understand it otherwise. You cannot understand God by shakings, and yet shakings may be in perfect order sometimes. But you can always tell when the Spirit moves and brings forth the utterances. They are always the utterances that magnify God. The Holy Spirit has a perfect plan. He comes right through every man who is so filled and brings divine utterances so that we may understand what the mind of the Lord is.

I will show you three passages in the Bible that pertain to the glory. The first is Psalm 16:9: *"Therefore my heart is glad, and my glory rejoices."* Something has made the rejoicing bring forth the glory. It was because his heart was glad.

"Glory and Virtue"

The second one is Psalm 108:1: *"O God, my heart is steadfast; I will sing and give praise, even with my glory."* You see, when the body is filled with the power of God, then the only thing that can express the glory is the tongue. Glory is presence, and the presence always comes by the tongue, which brings forth the revelations of God.

In Acts 2:25–26, we discover another aspect of this:

> *For David says concerning Him: "I foresaw the LORD always before my face, for He is at my right hand, that I may not be shaken. Therefore my heart rejoiced, and my tongue was glad."*

God first brings His power into us. Then He gives us verbal expressions by the same Spirit, the outward manifestation of what is within us. *"Out of the abundance of the heart the mouth speaks"* (Matt. 12:34).

Virtue has to be transmitted, and glory has to be expressed. Therefore, by filling us with the Holy Spirit, God has brought into us this glory so that out of us may come forth the glory. The Holy Spirit understands everything Christ has in the glory and brings through the heart of man God's latest thought. The world's needs, our manifestations, revivals, and all conditions are first settled in heaven, then worked out on the earth. We must be in touch with God Almighty in order to bring out on the face of the earth all the things that God has in the heavens. This is an ideal for us, and may God help us not to forsake the reality of holy communion with Him, of entering into private prayer so that publicly He may manifest His glory.

We must see the face of the Lord and understand His workings. There are things that God says to me that I know must take place. It does not matter what people say. I have been face to face with some of the most trying moments of men's lives, times when it made all the difference if I kept the vision and held fast to what God had said. A man must have immovable faith, and the voice of God must mean more to him than what he sees, feels, or what people say. He must have an originality born in heaven, transmitted or expressed in some way. We must bring heaven to earth.

Let us look again at 2 Peter 1:3: *"His divine power has given to us all things that pertain to life and godliness, through the knowledge of Him who called us by glory and virtue."* Oh, this is a lovely verse. There is so much depth in it for us. It is all real; it is all from heaven. It is as divinely appointed for this meeting as when the Holy Spirit was upon Peter. It is life to me. It is like the breath; it moves me. I must live in this grace. *"His divine power,"* there it is again, *"has given to us all things that pertain to life and godliness."* Oh, what wonderful things He has given us, *"through the knowledge of Him who called us by glory and virtue."* You cannot get away from Him. He is the center of all things. He moves the earth and transforms beings. He can live in every mind, plan every thought. Oh, He is there all the time.

You will find that Paul was full of the might of the Spirit breathing through him, and yet he came to a place where he felt he must stop. For there are greater things than he could utter even by prayer, when the Almighty breathes through the human soul.

At the end of Ephesians 3 are words that no human could ever think or write on his own. This passage is so mighty, so of God when it speaks about His being able to do all things, *"exceedingly abundantly above all that we ask or think"* (v. 20). The mighty God of revelation! The Holy Spirit gave these words of grandeur to stir our hearts, to move our affections, to transform us altogether. This is ideal! This is God. Shall we teach them? Shall we have them? Oh, they are ours. God has never put anything up on a pole where you could not reach it. He has brought His plan down to man, and if we are prepared, oh, what there is for us! I feel sometimes that we have just as much as we can digest. Yet such divine nuggets of precious truth are held before our hearts that it makes us understand that there are yet heights and depths and lengths and breadths of the knowledge of God stored up for us. (See Ephesians 3:17–19.) We might truly say,

> My heavenly bank, my heavenly bank,
> The house of God's treasure and store.
> I have plenty in here; I'm a real millionaire.

Glory! It is wonderful to never be poverty-stricken anymore, to have an inward knowledge of a bank that is greater than the Rothschilds, or any other wealthy person, has ever known about. It is stored up, nugget upon nugget—weights of glory, expressions of the invisible Christ to be seen by men.

God is shaking the earth to its foundations and causing us to understand that there is a principle in the Scriptures that may bring to man freedom from the natural order, and bring him into a place of holiness, righteousness, and the peace of God that passes all human understanding (Phil. 4:7). We must reach it. Praise God! God has brought us here on purpose so we may enter that place. He has brought us here this morning, and you say, "How will I be able to get all that is stored up for me?" Brother, sister, I know no other way: *"A broken and a contrite heart; these, O God, You will not despise"* (Ps. 51:17).

What do you want? Be definite in your seeking. God knows what you need, and that one thing is for you this morning. Set it in your minds that you will know the powers of the world to come.

> *Ask, and it will be given to you; seek, and you will find; knock, and it will be opened to you. For everyone who asks receives, and he who seeks finds, and to him who knocks it will be opened.* (Matt. 7:7–8)

14

The Might of the Spirit

ur theme is power for service and power in service. This is a very wonderful subject, and we may not be able to cover it all today. But there is so much in it, which we are now comprehending, that was once obscure to us. There is much that we now know about, much that we are no longer groping around for, thinking about, or speaking as much about as something that is not yet quite clear. We are speaking of the things we do know and testifying to the things we have seen. Now we are on the Rock. We are coming to understand what Peter received on that memorable day when our Lord said to him, *"You are Peter, and on this rock I will build My church, and the gates of Hades shall not prevail against it"* (Matt. 16:18).

We are standing on the foundation: the Rock, Christ, the Word, the Living Word. The power is contained in substance there. Christ is the substance of our faith. He is the hope of our inheritance. He is the substance and sum of this whole conference we are attending. If we go outside of that, we will be altogether outside the plan of the great ideal of this conference, whose overall theme is "Christ the Center."

Let us look at a passage from the first chapter of Acts:

> *The former account I made, O Theophilus, of all that Jesus began both to do and teach, until the day in which He was taken up, after He through the Holy Spirit had given commandments to the apostles whom He had chosen, to whom He also presented Himself alive after His suffering by many infallible proofs, being seen by them during forty days and speaking of the things pertaining to the kingdom of God. And being assembled together with them, He commanded them not to depart from Jerusalem, but to wait for the Promise of the Father, "which," He said, "you have heard from Me; for John truly baptized with water, but you shall be baptized with the Holy Spirit not many days from now." Therefore, when they had come together, they asked Him, saying, "Lord, will You at this time restore the kingdom to Israel?" And He said to them, "It is not for you to know times or seasons which the Father has put in His own authority. But you shall receive power when the Holy Spirit has come upon you; and you shall be witnesses to Me in Jerusalem, and in all Judea and Samaria, and to the end of the earth."*
>
> (Acts 1:1–8)

"You shall receive power when the Holy Spirit has come upon you." Jesus lived in the knowledge of that power. The Spirit of the Lord was upon Him.

The Might of the Spirit

Some of the important truths that I want to deal with today, as God breathes through me, are the fact of the power being there within us, the fact of a knowledge of that power, the fact of the substance being there, and the fact of what is being created or breathed or formed in us by God Himself.

We have come into a new order. We are dwelling in a place where Christ is the whole substance, and where man is but the body or the clay. The body is the temple of the Holy Spirit (1 Cor. 6:19); within the temple, a living principle is laid down of rock, the Word of the living God. It is formed in us, and it is a thousand times mightier than the "self" in thought, in language, in activity, and in movement. There is an anointing, a force, a power mightier than dynamite that is stronger than the mightiest gun that has ever been made. It is able to resist the greatest pressure that the Devil can bring against it. Mighty power has no might against this almighty power. When we speak about evil power, we speak about mighty power. But when we speak about almighty power, we speak about a substance of rock dynamite that diffuses through a person and displays its might and brings everything else into insignificance.

I want you to think through what I am saying. I want us to be able to lay everything down on the Word. *"The people who know their God shall be strong, and carry out great exploits"* (Dan. 11:32). The Holy Spirit has come with one definite purpose, and that is to reveal to us the Father and the Son in all their different branches of helpfulness to humanity. The Spirit has come to display almighty power so that the weak may be made strong, and to bring to sickness such a manifestation of the blood of

Christ, of the Atonement on Calvary, that the evil power of disease is conquered and forced to leave.

HOLY BOLDNESS

In this baptism of the Holy Spirit, there is a holy boldness—not superstition, but a boldness that stands unflinchingly and truly on what the Word of God says. To have holy boldness is to live in the Holy Spirit, to get to know the principles that are worked out by Him. I must understand that Jesus lived in a blessed, sweet fellowship with His Father, and He worked and operated because His Father worked. I must live in the same way. I must learn that the blessed principles of divine order are in me and that, as long as self doesn't take over, I am living only for Him.

Jesus is, and always ought to be, preeminent. Then there is no fear. Perfect love, perfect knowledge of God, of Jesus, brings me into a state where I have no fear. (See 1 John 4:18.) I have entered a new order in which Christ is working in me and bringing every thought into subjection. (See 2 Corinthians 10:5.) He is transforming my desires into what God desires, into a divine plan. Now I am working within a new plan in which self ceases, Christ does the work, and the work is accomplished.

"How does this happen?" you might be asking. I am going to mention a few things that will be helpful to you regarding this. You cannot have holy boldness unless you know God; do not attempt to exercise it unless you know Him. Daniel would never have survived the lions' den if he had not known God. What did the king say? He said, *"Daniel, servant of the living God, has your God, whom you serve continually,*

been able to deliver you from the lions?" (Dan. 6:20).
Daniel answered, *"O king, live forever! My God sent
His angel and shut the lions' mouths, so that they
have not hurt me"* (vv. 21–22).

In one sense, the mouths of the lions were shut
when Daniel was in the den, and yet, in another
sense, they were shut even before that. The lions'
mouths were shut when the decree forbidding prayer
to anyone except the king was signed and when
Daniel trusted in God to deliver him. (See Daniel
6:1–23.) You will always find that victory occurs at
the moment you open the door of your heart to believing.

I arrived one day in a place where there was a
great deal of strife and friction. I had a letter of introduction to a man there who was a stranger to me;
I did not know a single person in town. I brought the
letter to this man, and when he had read it, he said,
"This letter is from Brother ——— of Cleveland. I
know him. The letter mentions much about you.
There will be an open door for you here." Immediately, he added, "Go out and visit these people"—he
gave me their names—"and then come back to din
ner." I got back a little bit late, and as soon as I arrived, he said, "I am sorry you are late for dinner.
We have already had dinner, for this reason: A
heartbroken young man has been here. He was going
to marry a beautiful young woman. But she is dying,
and the doctor is by her side and cannot help her.
That young man has promised to be here and will be
here in a minute. You had better get ready." I replied, "I am ready now."

Just as I started to eat my dinner, in came this
brokenhearted man. I did not question him. I went

with him, and we arrived at the house where the young woman was. Her mother met me at the door, brokenhearted. I said to her, "Cheer up. Show me the girl; take me to her. It will be all right in a minute or two." Right away, I was taken into the house and upstairs. The young woman lay there in bed. She was suffering greatly from acute appendicitis. I said to her, "It will be all right in a minute or two." Then I said, "Come out!" and instantly she was healed. That was holy boldness!

What do I mean by holy boldness? We may say that there is a divine position where a person may dwell and where he has such a knowledge of God that he knows God will not fail him. It is not a miracle, although at times it almost seems as if it has a measure of the miraculous. At times it does not act exactly as the human mind would like it to act. God does not act in that way. He very often acts in quite an opposite way.

What I want you to know is that God has a plan for His children. What happened in that case I just mentioned? There is the secret. The doctor came a short time after that girl had been healed, and he could not understand it. He saw this young woman; she was dressed and downstairs ten minutes after having been made well. Meanwhile, during the time it took her to dress, another four people were definitely healed. What was God's purpose? That young doctor had been investigating the power of healing, and he had not been able to find a single person who was able to heal in this way. He called to the young woman, "Are you downstairs?" "Yes," she replied. "Come here," he said. The young woman said, "A young man"—she called me a young man—"from

England has been brought, and I was instantly healed." "Come here," he repeated. Then he pressed his long finger into the soft part of that tumor. It would have made her scream if she had still had appendicitis. But he could not find any symptoms, and he said, "This is God. This is God."

Did anything else happen in that town? Yes. They had built a new meetinghouse there, but it had never been filled to capacity. But the leader said, "I am going to prophesy that there will be so many people, our place won't be able to hold them." And that's exactly the way it was. Did anything else happen? Yes, God healed over two hundred people in that place. Brothers and sisters, it is not we who do this. I am very aware of the fact that it is just as Jesus said in John 14:10, *"The words that I speak to you I do not speak on My own authority; but the Father who dwells in Me does the works."* Is that not beautiful? Just think of it, some of you who have been so busy in arranging plans for preaching. Think of how wonderful it is when the Holy Spirit comes and takes possession of you and speaks through you just the things that are needed.

Some people say, "Do these things last?" Praise God, His truth never fails to last; it goes on lasting. I received a letter the other day from Albany, Oregon, which is about seventy miles south of Portland. This person had not written to me since I visited there. The letter ran like this: "Do you remember my taking you to my wife's brother, who had lost all power of reason and everything? [Alcohol and the power of the Devil had taken hold of him.] My brother-in-law has been perfectly whole ever since, and has not tasted alcohol."

"You shall receive power" (Acts 1:8). Glory to God. I have come to understand that if I will be still, God can work; if I will be sure that I pay the price and do not come out of the divine order, God will certainly work.

Let me say a word to your hearts. Most of us here today are diligently seeking God's best. We feel that we would pay any price for His best. God knows my heart. I do not have an atom of desire outside the perfect will of God, and God knows this. But Wigglesworth, like everybody else, occasionally has to ask, "What is wrong with me? I do not feel the anointing," and if there is anything to repent of, I get right down before God and get it out. You cannot cover over sins; you cannot cover over faults. You must get to the bottom of them. I cannot have the anointing, the power of the Holy Spirit, the life of Christ, and the manifest glory except through self-abasement and complete renunciation of self—with God alone enthroned and Wigglesworth dead to himself. It must be of God, and if a person will only examine the conditions and act upon them, I tell you, things will come off wonderfully.

Interpretation of Tongues

The deliverances of the Lord are as high as the righteousness of heaven, the purity of His saints is as white as linen, and the divine principles of His gracious will can only flow out when He is enthroned within. Christ first, last; always Christ. Through Christ and by the name of Jesus, "whatever you shall ask in My name I will do."

The Might of the Spirit

I repeat: people sometimes say, "Do these things last; is this thing permanent?" The baptism of the Holy Spirit in my life is like a river flowing on. It has been eight years since I was baptized in the Holy Spirit, and the tide rises higher and higher. Holiness, purity of heart, divine thoughts, and revelations of God are far in advance of what they were even a short time ago.

We are living in a divine place where the Lord is blessedly having His way. I want you to hear what I have to say about one or two more things. Some people can have things rubbed out of their lives, but I want God Almighty to do something now that cannot be rubbed out. We are definitely told in the Word of God that if we ask God for the Holy Spirit, He will give Him (Luke 11:13). We hear people say this quite easily, but I find that many people who dwell on this promise do not receive the baptism. I know when a person is baptized in the Holy Spirit. There is a kindred spirit with a person who is baptized in the Holy Spirit that is not there with any other person.

The Holy Spirit is given to those who obey. To those who obey what? What Jesus said. What did Jesus say? *"Tarry...until you are endued with power from on high"* (Luke 24:49). Is that not clear? That is Scripture. You do not need to have anything more scriptural than that.

Now, the reason why God the Holy Spirit brings me into this place today is that I love the church of God. When I hear men and women who are as saved as I am speaking in a way that I know is not according to the Spirit of God, I know exactly of what spirit they are. May God save us from building on our own imaginations. Let us build on what the

Word of God says. We will never be strong unless we believe what God says. If God tells me in His Word that Paul was the chief of sinners (1 Tim. 1:15), I say I will believe it; I will believe it forever. Whatever the Holy Spirit says through His Word, I believe it and keep to it. I will not move from it. And in Acts 1:8, the Holy Spirit says I will have power after He comes upon me through Jesus.

Interpretation of Tongues

They who fear the Lord and they who keep His commandments will have the goodness of the land; and they who will do His will will know the doctrine, and God will declare unto their hearts the perfectness of His way. For "there is a way that seems right to a man, but the way of that is death"; but the way of righteousness brings to pass that God's Word is true.

FIND YOUR PLACE IN THE HOLY SPIRIT

I am so pleased because there is a thought coming into my heart that all of you ought to know. I believe there is a great need today for us to find our place in the Holy Spirit. It would save us from so many burdens and many other things. I am going to give you a little illustration of this. There is a dear woman who lives at our house and who looks after my affairs. She perpetually makes herself a real slave-servant. I often think she does so much that is not needed. She is a slave-servant; that is her disposition. There are many people like this. Now, we have many people in our meetings whom God has been blessing and who have gone out to speak for Him in different places. This woman thought she ought to do the same. We had received many invitations for people to speak, and she accepted one of these invitations. She looked timid but said she had to lead this service. I got up with the needed boldness and set to work to strip away what was causing this timidity. With her heart full, she went out and found someone else to lead the meeting, and instantly she found relief. She came back with her face beaming. "What's up?" I asked. She said, "I've found relief." The burden was gone.

Some people, just because they have been baptized with the Holy Spirit and with fire (Matt. 3:11), think they have to go and be preachers. It is a pity— it is a thousand pities—that it is so. It is good that such a desire is in your heart, but it may not be God's purpose for you. If you would get to know your place in the Holy Spirit, it would save you from struggles and burdens and would relieve the whole situation. Get to know your place in the Holy Spirit, and God will bless you. There are people here whose hearts are crushed because they are not able to sing as well as our Welsh brother can. But it would not do for every one of us to be like him. We would be breaking all the glass in the place if we were all like him. We all have to get to know our positions in the Holy Spirit. God can work it so beautifully and harmonize it so that nothing will be out of order.

God will put you in the place you are to occupy if you will ask and trust Him for it. Then you will live in the Holy Spirit so that His glory will always be upon you. If you miss it, say, like David, "Lord, *'restore to me the joy of Your salvation'*" (Ps. 51:12).

If you feel out of touch with God, get back to Calvary; keep near the Cross. Let the God of Glory glorify Himself in you.

It is marvelous how all the gifts of the Spirit may be manifested in some people. Everybody acquainted with me knows that I used to be short of speech, slow at everything, and all out of order. My wife used to preach, and I carried the babies and the boots and everything. Then there came a time when my wife could not be there and I was forced to roll in somehow. Well, I rolled in, and I was very glad to roll out many times. But it is marvelous now. As a calling, God has allowed every one of the nine gifts of the Spirit to be ministered through me. (See 1 Corinthians 12:8–10.) There is not a single gift that has not been ministered through me. What I mean is this. You won't hear me say that I *have* these gifts. But, living in the Holy Spirit, I am in a place where God can manifest any gift at any moment that it is needed. You also may live in this glorious place. Then it is heaven to live, it is heaven to eat, it is heaven to sleep—it is heaven all the time. And when heaven comes, it will only be more fullness, for the kingdom of heaven is already within.

I am speaking from my heart this morning. It is no good for me to speak unless I speak from my heart. I have put my hands to this work, and I feel that God the Holy Spirit has done something, and I just want to speak about it in closing. I know you will believe it; I know it is true. God has helped me to go into different places and bring about revivals. Over and over again, revivals begin with people who are baptized in the Holy Spirit, and God does great things. Last night, there was a preacher here. There he was. He knelt down. He was as stiff as a board. You need to have discernment to see whether there is a real desire in people who are seeking the baptism. This preacher was frightened to let go. I said, "Come, brother, receive the Holy Spirit," and he replied, "I cannot." I told him, "You are not in earnest; you are not real. There is no resoluteness about you. You must begin to move. Receive the Holy Spirit." Then, when I knew that he was really being stirred up, according to God's divine order, I put my hands on him and said, "Receive the Holy Spirit." God the Holy Spirit shook him from top to bottom and inside out. What a wonderful baptism he had!

Brothers and sisters, do you want the Holy Spirit? We sing some hymns that speak of the breath of the Holy Spirit. In the Bible, we read that Jesus breathed upon His disciples, and they received the anointing in His breath (John 20:22). As people breathe in the Holy Spirit, they become so possessed with the power of God that they have no possessions in themselves. They simply fall into God, and God takes possession of everything—hands, feet, body, and tongue—for His glory. My heart yearns for you to be so filled with the divine power of the Holy Spirit that you will return to your own meetings and assemblies in the order of God. You are not to take any special notice of your fullness, but the fact will remain in you that you have the power of the Holy Spirit. Let the Word of God act upon this power in such a way that God will let it flow through you to others. In what way? In His way. You cannot baptize people, but He can do it. How? *"Receive the Holy Spirit"* (John 20:22). Let Him have His way.

15

The Place of Victory

oday I have been led to deal with an important truth that will be helpful for us in our Christian lives. The thought that has been pressing on my mind for some time is the thought of abiding in God. There is joy in being at the place where we can always count on being in the presence of Power—where we know that God's presence is with us, leading us to the place where victory is assured. This is the important truth that I have been led to think of. We are here to get hold of the thought that if we keep in the right place with God, God can do anything with us.

Let us look at a few passages of Scripture. The first is Luke 4:1–2: *"Then Jesus, being filled with the Holy Spirit, returned from the Jordan and was led by the Spirit into the wilderness, being tempted for forty days by the devil."* In Mark's account of Jesus' temptation, he spoke about Jesus being "driven" by the Spirit into the wilderness. (See Mark 1:12.)

Whatever Luke and Mark meant by Jesus being *"led"* or "driven" by the Holy Spirit, one thing is certain: a power, a majesty, had fallen on Jesus, and

He was no longer the same man. He had received this mighty anointing power of God, and He realized that the only thing for Him to do was to submit. As He submitted, He was more and more covered with the power and led by the Spirit. The Holy Spirit took Him away into the wilderness, with its darkness and great privations. For forty days He was without food, but because of the presence and the power within and on Him, He was certain of victory. With this power, He faced the wild beasts of the wilderness (Mark 1:13) and the lack of every human sustenance. Then, at the end of the forty days, in that holy attainment, He was brought into a state of persecution and trial such as a man likely has never been attacked by before or since.

In that place of persecution and trial, God sustained Him mightily. With what did God sustain Him? With this holy, blessed anointing. I want you to really think about this. God sustained Jesus with the holy, blessed anointing that was upon Him and that so brought the Word of God to bear upon Satan that Jesus was like the *"pen of a ready writer"* (Ps. 45:1) and slew Satan every time with God's Word.

Let us look at another passage of Scripture. In Luke 4:14–15, you will see that *"Jesus returned in the power of the Spirit to Galilee, and news of Him went out through all the surrounding region. And He taught in their synagogues, being glorified by all."* I want you to understand that after the trials, after all the temptations, and everything else, He came out more full of God, more clothed with the Spirit, and more ready for the fight. The endowment with power had such an effect on Him that other people saw it and flocked to hear Him, and great blessings came to the land. He was among His kinsfolk and relatives, and in the spirit of this kind of holy attainment, He went into the synagogue. He was given a scroll of the Scriptures, and He read, *"The Spirit of the LORD is upon Me, because He has anointed Me to preach the gospel to the poor"* (Luke 4:18).

I want you to keep in mind where the anointing came from. How was Jesus anointed? How did it come to Him? You remember how that came about: *"Jesus also was baptized; and while He prayed, the heaven was opened. And the Holy Spirit descended in bodily form like a dove upon Him"* (Luke 3:21–22). In just the same manner, I see that the Holy Spirit also fell upon the disciples at Pentecost. (See Acts 2:1–4.) I see that they were anointed with the same power; I see that they went forth, and success attended their ministry until the power of God swept through the whole earth. I want you to see that it was because of this anointing, this power, that when Peter and John spoke to the lame man at the gate of the temple, the man was able to rise and leap for joy. (See Acts 3:1–8.)

The Holy Spirit coming upon an individual is capable of changing him, fertilizing his spiritual life, and filling him with such power and grace that he wouldn't be able to say that anything was impossible but that all things are possible with God (Matt. 19:26). What could happen, what is possible, if we reach this place and stay in it—if we abide in it? Some people have an idea that they have to be doing something. I implore you, by the power of the Holy Spirit, that you see that there is only one thing that is going to accomplish the purposes of God, and that is being in the Spirit. I don't care how dry the land is. I don't care how thirsty the land is. I don't care how many or how few vessels are available. I implore you, in the name of Jesus, to keep in the Spirit. That's the secret.

Now, let us go to the book of Ezekiel. The Lord asked the prophet Ezekiel, *"Son of man, can these bones live?"* (Ezek. 37:3). He answered, *"O Lord GOD, You know"* (v. 3). When you are in the Spirit and the dry bones surround you and barren conditions are all around you; when you think everything is exactly the opposite of your desires and you can see no deliverance by human power; then, knowing that your condition is known to God and that God wants men and women who are willing to submit and submit and yield and yield to the Holy Spirit until their bodies are saturated and soaked with God, you realize that God your Father has you in such a condition that, at any moment, He can reveal His will to you.

I want you to understand that there is something more in this. I want you to see that God is everything to us. I believe that we have come to a place where we have to submit ourselves to the mighty anointing power of God and where we will see that we are in the will of God. I pray to God the Holy Spirit that if He does one thing among us today, it will be to show us our leanness and our distance from this place. It is not that we are not contending for it, but what we need is a great hunger and thirst for God.

Ezekiel said, *"O dry bones, hear the word of the LORD!"* (v. 4). I would like you to understand that God spoke first. He spoke so loudly and clearly and so distinctly that this man, Ezekiel, who was filled with the Spirit, heard every word. I want you to understand that there was not any movement in that valley of dry bones; until the word of the Lord was spoken by the prophet, the bones were as dry as at the beginning. God had spoken, and the message had gone forth. But nothing had yet happened. What was the matter? Ah! It was only that the word of God needed to go forth through His servant the prophet. The world has to be brought to a knowledge of the truth, but this will only be brought about through human instrumentality. This will occur when the human instrument is at a place where he will say all that the Holy Spirit directs him to say.

Ezekiel rose up and, clothed with divine power, began to speak; he began to prophesy. Then there was a rattling among the bones; bone came together with bone at the voice of the man filled with the Spirit of the living God. God had given him the victory. God wants to give us the victory in a similar way.

What does the Word say? *"Be still, and know that I am God"* (Ps. 46:10). This is the place of tranquility, where we know that He is controlling and moving us by the mighty power of His Spirit. Beloved, this is the place that we need to reach. This prophecy is for us. Truly, God wants to begin this in us. There are many dry places. What does that have to do with you? You are to be the Lord's instrument. *"The Lord's hand is not shortened, that it cannot save"* (Isa. 59:1). Man's extremity is God's opportunity; His Word will awaken to meet the need. *"All things are possible to him who believes"* (Mark 9:23). But if we are to do the will of God at the right time and place, we must get into the Spirit and, in so doing, give God a fair chance.

Ezekiel said, *"So I prophesied as I was commanded"* (Ezek. 37:7). He did just what he was told to do. It takes more to live in that place than any other that I know of—to live in the place where you hear God's voice. It is only by the power of the Holy Spirit that you can quickly do as you are told. Ezekiel continued, *"And as I prophesied, there was a noise, and suddenly a rattling; and the bones came together, bone to bone"* (v. 7). There is something worth your notice in this. It is only the Spirit who can make what is crooked straight. (See Isaiah 42:16.) Only yield so that He may have full control of all that you are. We must get to the place where we will see God and know His voice when He sends us with a message that brings life, power, and victory.

What happened when the prophet spoke the word of the Lord? *"And breath came into them, and they lived, and stood upon their feet, an exceedingly great army"* (Ezek. 37:10).

16

"The Best with Improvement"

et the Spirit cover you today so that you may be intensely earnest about the deep things of God. You should be so in the order of the Spirit that you may know this: that your will, your mind, and your heart may be so centered in God that He may lift you into the pavilion of splendor where you hear His voice—lift you to the place where the breath of the Almighty can send you to pray and send you to preach, the Spirit of the Lord being upon you.

You are at God's banquet, a banquet at which you are never separated from Him and He multiplies spiritual blessings and fruit in your life. It is a banquet where you have to increase with all increasing, where God has for you riches beyond all things—not fleshly things, not carnal things, but spiritual manifestations, gifts, fruits of the Spirit, and beautiful beatitudes, the blessing of God always being upon you. (See 2 Corinthians 9:10–11.)

Are you ready to enter into this glorious place where you no longer live for yourself? God will take over your life and send you out to win thousands of people to Christ, so that they also may enter into eternal grace.

Interpretation of Tongues

The Spirit moves and changes His operation, bringing the soul into the place of hunger and desire until the whole of the being "cries out for the living God." Truly the creature must be delivered from this present evil thing. So God is operating through us by these meetings and letting us know that "all flesh is grass." But He is bringing the Spirit of revelation, that we may know that this inheritance we are having is to endure forever and ever, for we belong to the new creation of God, clothed upon with the Spirit, made like unto Him, because our whole hearts now are bringing forth what God has established. It is out of the fullness of the truth of the hidden heart that God flows forth His glory, His power—His might and His revelation and His power in association—and makes us one and says, "You are Mine."

For our study, the Lord has led me to select the first chapter of James. This is a marvelous subject in itself. This is the Master's subject, and He will be able to manage it. I would have to give up if it were my subject, but seeing it is the Master's subject, I will begin.

"The Best with Improvement"

James, a bondservant of God and of the Lord Jesus Christ, to the twelve tribes which are scattered abroad: Greetings. My brethren, count it all joy when you fall into various trials. (James 1:1–2)

VICTORIOUS IN BATTLE

No person is ever able to talk about victory over temptation unless he goes through it. All the victories are won in battles.

There are tens of thousands of people in Europe, America, and in other parts of the world, who wear badges to show they have been in battle, and they rejoice in it. They would be ashamed to wear such badges if they had not been in battle. The battle is what gives them the right to wear the badge.

It is those who have been in the fight who can tell about the victories. It is those who have been tried to the utmost who can come out and tell you a story about it. It was only James and Peter and Paul, those who were in the front lines of the battle, who told us how we have to rejoice in our trials because wonderful blessings will come out of them. It is in the trials that we are made.

TRIBULATION, PATIENCE, EXPERIENCE

You want a spiritual experience, do you? Read this Scripture passage; it will give you an experience. I know nothing like it:

Therefore being justified by faith, we have peace with God through our Lord Jesus

Christ: by whom also we have access by faith into this grace wherein we stand, and rejoice in hope of the glory of God. And not only so, but we glory in tribulations also: knowing that tribulation worketh patience; and patience, experience. (Rom. 5:1–4 KJV)

And out of the experience, we tell what is being done in our lives. Do you want to have a big story to tell? Well, it is here: *"Count it all joy"* (James 1:2) in the midst of temptations. When the trial is severe; when you think that no one is being tried as much as you; when you feel as if some strange thing has happened (1 Pet. 4:12) so that you are altogether in a new order; when the trial is so hard you cannot sleep and you do not know what to do; *"count it all joy."* God has something in it, something of a divine nature. You are in a good place when you do not know what to do.

After Abraham was tried, he could offer Isaac, but not before he was tried. God put him through all kinds of tests. For twenty-five years, he was tested, and he was called "the father of the faithful" (see Romans 4:9–16) because he would not give in. We have blessing today because one man dared to believe God for twenty-five years without budging.

LIVING IN FAITH FOR TWELVE MONTHS

A woman came up to me in a meeting one day and said, "I have come for you to heal me. Can you see this big goiter?"

"I can hardly see anything else," I answered.

"The Best with Improvement"

She had told her father and mother and the rest of her family before she came that she believed she was going to be healed because Wigglesworth was going to pray for her. As soon as she was prayed for, we had a testimony meeting. Her testimony was wonderful. "Oh!" she said. "I thank God because He has perfectly healed me!" She went home, and they were all glad to hear what she said. "When I was prayed for, I was perfectly healed!" she exultantly exclaimed.

For twelve months, she went everywhere among the assemblies, telling how God had healed her. After those twelve months, I returned to the same place to hold meetings, and she came again, filled with joy. When she came in, the people said, "Look who's here. Oh, look how big that goiter is!" They were all staring at her.

After a while, we had a testimony meeting. "Twelve months ago," she said, "I was prayed for here, and I was marvelously healed. I have had twelve months of the most wonderful time on earth because God so wonderfully healed me twelve months ago."

After the meeting, she went home. When she got there, she said to her mother, "Oh, if you had been there and seen the people, how they were moved when they heard me tell how God healed me."

"Look," the mother said, "you don't know—you don't seem to know—but the people are believing there is something wrong with your mind, and they believe the entire family is affected by it, as well! You are bringing disgrace upon the whole family. It is shameful. We are disgusted with you. The whole thing is being rolled onto us because you are not right in the head. Why don't you go look in the mirror, and you will see that the thing has not moved at all."

She went to her room and prayed, "Lord, I do not want to look in the mirror. I believe You have done it, but let all the people know that You have done it. Let them all know that You have done it, just the same as You have let me know it." The next morning, she came downstairs as perfect as anybody could be, and the family knew that the Lord had done it.

"MORE PRECIOUS THAN GOLD"

Some of you wonder what is up when you are not healed in a moment. God never breaks His promise. The trial of your faith is *"much more precious than gold"* (1 Pet. 1:7).

God has you on this earth for the purpose of bringing out His character in you. He wants to destroy the power of the Devil. He wants to move you so that in the face of difficulties and hardships, you will praise the Lord. *"Count it all joy"* (James 1:2). You have to take a leap today; you have to leap into the promises. You have to believe that God never fails you; you have to believe it is impossible for God to break His word. He is *"from everlasting to everlasting"* (Ps. 90:2).

> Forever and ever, not for a day,
> He keepeth His promise forever;
> To all who believe,
> To all who obey,
> He keepeth His promise forever.

"The Best with Improvement"

There is no variableness with God; there is no *"shadow of turning"* (James 1:17). He is the same. He manifests His divine glory.

Jesus said to Mary and Martha, *"If you would believe you would see the glory of God"* (John 11:40). We must understand that there will be times of testing, but they are only to make us more like the Master. He was *"in all points tempted as we are, yet without sin"* (Heb. 4:15). He endured all things. He is our example.

Oh, that God would place us in an earnest, intent position in which flesh and blood have to yield to the Spirit of God! We will go forward; we will not be moved by our feelings.

Suppose that a man who is prayed for today gets a blessing, but tomorrow he begins murmuring because he does not feel exactly as he ought to feel. What is he doing? He is replacing the Word of God with his feelings. What an awful disgrace it is for you to replace the Word of God with your feelings. Let God have His perfect work.

"My brethren, count it all joy" (James 1:2). This does not mean "Count a bit of it as joy" but *"count it all joy."* It doesn't matter from what source the trial comes, whether it is your business or your home or what. *"Count it all joy."* Why? Because *"we know that all things work together for good to those who love God, to those who are the called according to His purpose"* (Rom. 8:28).

That is a great Scripture. It means that you have a special position. God is electrifying the very position that you hold so that the Devil will see that you have a godly character, and he will have to say about you what he said about Job.

Recall the scene. God asked, "Satan, what is your opinion about Job?" Then the Lord went on and said, "Don't you think he is wonderful? Don't you think he is the most excellent man in all the earth?"

Satan replied, "Yes, but You know, You are keeping him."

Praise the Lord! I am glad the Devil has to tell the truth. And don't you know that God can keep you, also?

"If You touch everything he has," the Devil said, "he will curse You to Your face."

God answered, "You can touch all he has, but you cannot touch him." (See Job 1:8–12.)

The Scripture says that Jesus was dead but is alive again and has power over death and hell. To this, the Scripture adds a big *"Amen"* (Rev. 1:18). The Devil cannot take your life unless the Lord allows it. "You cannot touch Job's life," God told Satan. (See Job 2:6.)

Satan thought he could destroy Job, and you know the calamity that befell this righteous man. But Job said, *"Naked I came from my mother's womb, and naked shall I return there....Blessed be the name of the LORD"* (Job 1:21). Oh, it is lovely! The Lord can give us that kind of language. It is not the language of the head. This is divine language; this is heart acquaintance.

I want you to know that we can have heart acquaintance. It is far more for me to speak out of the abundance of my heart than out of the abundance of my head. I learned a long time ago that libraries often create swelled heads, but nothing except the Library, the Bible, can make swelled hearts. You are to have swelled hearts because out of the heart full of the fragrance of the love of God, the living life of the Lord flows.

Interpretation of Tongues

It is the Spirit who gives liberty. The prophet is nothing, but the Spirit brings us into attainment where we sit at His feet and seek with Him and have communications of things divine. For now we are not belonging to the earth; we are "transformed by the renewing of our mind" and "set in heavenly places with Christ Jesus."

You must cease to be. That is a difficult thing—for both you and me—but it is no trouble at all when you are in the hands of the Potter. You are only wrong when you are kicking. You are all right when you are still and He is forming you afresh. So let Him form you afresh today into a new vessel so that you will stand the stress.

BE PERFECT

"But let patience have its perfect work, that you may be perfect" (James 1:4).

Is this possible? Certainly, it is possible. Who was speaking in this verse? It was the breath of the Spirit; it was also the hidden man of the heart who had a heart like his Brother. This was James, the Lord's brother, who was speaking. He spoke very much like his Brother. When we read these wonderful words, we might very likely be encountering a true kindred spirit with Christ.

James had to learn patience. It was not an easy thing for him to understand how his Brother could be the Son of God and be in the same family as he, Judas, and the other brothers. (See Matthew 13:55.) It was not an easy thing for him, and he had to learn to be patient to see how it worked out.

There are many things in your life that you cannot understand. But be patient, for when the hand of God is upon something, it may grind very slowly, but it will form the finest thing possible if you dare to wait until it is completed. Do not kick until you have gone through the process—and when you are dead enough to yourself, you will never kick at all. It is a death we die so that we might be alive unto God. It is only by the deaths we die that we are able to be still before God.

Jesus said, "The cross? I can endure the cross. The shame? I can despise it." (See Hebrews 12:2.) He withstood the bitter language spoken to Him at the cross: "If You are the Christ, come down, and we will believe." (See Matthew 27:40, 42.) They struck Him, but He *"did not revile in return"* (1 Pet. 2:23).

He is the picture for us. Why did He do it? He was patient. Why? He knew that when He came to the uttermost end of the Cross, He would forever save all those who would believe.

You cannot tell what God has in mind for you. As you are still before God—pliable in His hands— He will be working out a greater vessel than you could ever imagine in all your life.

"COMPLETE, LACKING NOTHING"

"Let patience have its perfect work, that you may be perfect and complete, lacking nothing" (James

1:4). To be *"complete"* means that you are not moved by anything, that you are living only in the divine position of God. It means that you are not moved, that you are not changed by what people say. There is something about divine acquaintance that is instilled; it is worked within a person by the mighty God. It becomes like intuition.

The new life of God is not just on the surface. It builds the character of a person in purity until his inward heart is filled with divine love and has nothing but thoughts of God alone. *"That you may be perfect and complete, lacking nothing."*

When I was in New Zealand, some people came to me and said, "We would like to give you a Christmas present, if you can tell us what you would like." "I haven't a desire in the world," I said. "I cannot tell you anything I would like. I have no desire for anything except God."

One day, I was walking down the street with a millionaire. I was feeling wonderfully happy over the way the Lord was blessing in our meetings. As we walked together, I said, "Brother, I haven't a care in the world. I am as happy as a bird!"

"Oh!" he said. "Stop! Say it again! Say it again!" And he stood still, waiting for me to repeat it. "Brother, I haven't a care in the world. I am as happy as a bird!" He exclaimed, "I would give all my money, I would give everything I have, to have that!"

To be lacking nothing—hallelujah!

The Spirit of the Lord is moving us mightily to see that this is resurrection power. We were planted with Him, and we have been raised with Him (Rom. 6:5 KJV). We are from above (see Colossians 3:1–3);

we do not belong to what is below. We *"reign in life"* (Rom. 5:17) by Another. It is the life of God's Son manifested in this human body.

ASK GOD FOR WISDOM

"If any of you lacks wisdom, let him ask of God, who gives to all liberally and without reproach, and it will be given to him" (James 1:5). This is a very remarkable Scripture. Many people come to me and ask if I will pray for them to have faith. I want to encourage them, but I cannot depart from God's Word. I cannot grant people faith. But by the power of the Spirit, I can stimulate you until you dare to believe and rest on the authority of God's Word. The Spirit of the living God quickens you, and I see that *"faith comes by hearing, and hearing by the word of God"* (Rom. 10:17).

This is a living word of faith: *"If any of you lacks wisdom, let him ask of God, who gives to all liberally."* You will never find that God ever judges you for the wisdom He gives you or for the blessing He gives you. He makes it so that when you come to Him again, He gives again, never asking what you did with what He gave you before. That is the way God gives. God *"gives to all liberally and without reproach."* So you have a chance today to come for much more. Do you want wisdom? Ask of God.

Interpretation of Tongues

It is not the wisdom that you get from the earth: it is divine wisdom. It brings a peaceful position; it rules with diligence, and it causes you to live in quietness. You know the difference between the "wisdom that is from above" and the wisdom that is from below, and so the Spirit breathes through our brother to show you that you have to be so in the perfect will of God in asking for these things until one thing must be fulfilled in your heart: if you ask, you must believe, for God is only pleased when you believe.

You have to be in the right condition for asking. This is the condition: *"But let him ask in faith, with no doubting"* (James 1:6).

I am satisfied that God, who is the builder of divine order, never brings confusion into His order. It is only when things are out of order that God brings confusion. God brought confusion upon the men who were building the Tower of Babel because they were out of order. (See Genesis 11:1–9.) What were they doing? They were trying to get into heaven by a way that was not God's way, and they were thieves and robbers. (See John 10:1.) So He turned their language to confusion. There is a way into the kingdom of heaven, and it is through the blood of the Lord Jesus Christ.

If you want this divine order in your life, if you want wisdom, you have to come to God believing. I want to impress upon you the fact—and I am learning it more every day—that if you ask six times for anything, just for the sake of asking, it shows you are an unbelieving person. If you really believe, you will ask God and know that He has abundance for your every need. But if you go right in the face of belief and ask six times, He knows very well that you do not mean what you ask, so you do not get it. God does not honor unbelief; He honors faith.

If you would really get down to business about the baptism of the Holy Spirit and ask God once and definitely to fill you, believing it, what would you do? You would begin to praise Him for it because you would know He had given it.

If you ask God once for healing, you will get it. But if you ask a thousand times a day until you do not even know you are asking, you will get nothing. If you would ask God for your healing now and begin praising Him because He never breaks His word, you would go out of here perfect. *"Only believe"* (Mark 5:36).

God wants to promote us. He wants us to get away from our own thoughts and our own foolishness, and get to a definite place, believing that He exists and that *"He is a rewarder of those who diligently seek Him"* (Heb. 11:6).

Have you gotten to the place where you dare to do this? Have you gotten to the place where you are no longer going to murmur when you are undergoing a trial? Are you going to go around weeping, telling people about it, or are you going to say, "Thank you, Lord, for putting me on the top"?

A great number of ministers and evangelists do not get checks sent to them any longer because they didn't thank the donor for the last one. Many people receive no blessing because they did not thank God for the last blessing. A thankful heart is a receiving heart. God wants to keep you in the place of constant believing.

> Keep on believing, Jesus is near,
> Keep on believing, there's nothing to fear;
> Keep on believing, this is the way,
> Faith in the night, the same as the day.

ENDURED TEMPTATION BRINGS THE CROWN

"Blessed is the man who endures temptation; for when he has been approved, he will receive the crown of life" (James 1:12). People do not know what they are getting when they are in a great place of temptation. Temptation endured brings the *"crown of life."*

> *He will receive the crown of life which the Lord has promised to those who love Him. Let no one say when he is tempted, "I am tempted by God"; for God cannot be tempted by evil, nor does He Himself tempt anyone. But each one is tempted when he is drawn away by his own desires and enticed. Then, when desire has conceived, it gives birth to sin; and sin, when it is full-grown, brings forth death. Do not be deceived, my beloved brethren.*
>
> *(James 1:12–16)*

There is nothing outside of purity except what is sin. All unbelief is sin. God wants you to have a pure, active faith so that you will be living in an advanced place of believing God all the time, and so that you will be on the mountaintop and singing when other people are crying.

I want to speak now about lust. I am not speaking about the base things, the carnal desires. I am not speaking so much about adultery, fornication, and such things, but I am speaking about what has turned you aside to some other thing instead of God. God has been offering you better things all the time, and you have missed them.

There are three things in life, and I notice that many people are satisfied with just one of them. There is blessing in justification, there is blessing in sanctification, and there is blessing in the baptism of the Holy Spirit. Salvation is a wonderful thing, and we know it. Sanctification is a process that takes us on to a higher level with God. Salvation, sanctification, and the fullness of the Spirit are processes.

Many people are satisfied with "good"—that is, with salvation. Other people are satisfied with "better"—a sanctified life, purified by God. Still other people are satisfied with the "best"—the fullness of God with revelation from on high. I am not satisfied with any of the three. I am only satisfied with the "best with improvement."

So I come to you not with good, but better; not with better, but best; not with best, but best with improvement—going on with God. Why? Because *"when desire has conceived, it gives birth to sin; and sin, when it is full-grown, brings forth death"* (James 1:15). When anything has taken me from God, it means death in some way.

When Jesus said to the disciples, "The Son of Man will be put into the hands of sinners and crucified," Peter rebuked Him (see Matthew 16:21–22), but Jesus said, *"Get behind Me, Satan! You are an offense to Me, for you are not mindful of the things of God, but the things of men"* (v. 23).

Anything that hinders me from denying myself and taking up my cross (v. 24) is of the Devil; anything that hinders me from being separated unto God is of the Devil; and anything that hinders me from being purified every day is carnal, and it is death. So I implore you today to make certain that there is no lustful thing in you that would rob you of the glory. Then God will take you to the very summit of the blessing where you can be increased day by day into all His fullness.

Here is another Scripture I want you to receive. I understand clearly by this that God has worked out the whole plan of our inheritance. He is showing us that the whole thing is so beautiful and that we are brought into existence in the spiritual order through the Word:

> *So then, my beloved brethren, let every man be swift to hear, slow to speak, slow to wrath; for the wrath of man does not produce the righteousness of God. Therefore lay aside all filthiness and overflow of wickedness, and receive with meekness the implanted word, which is able to save your souls.* *(James 1:19–21)*

Do not neglect the Word of God. Take time to think about the Word of God; it is the only place of safety.

17

Unconditional Surrender

t is Pentecost that has made me rejoice in Jesus. God has been confirming His power by His Holy Spirit. I have an intense yearning to see Pentecost, and I am not seeing it. I may feel a little of the glow, but what we need is a deeper work of the Holy Spirit in order for God's message to come full of life and power and sharper than a *"two edged sword"* (Heb. 4:12). At Pentecost, Peter stood up in the power of the Holy Spirit, and three thousand people were saved. Not long after this, he preached again, and five thousand people were saved.

I am positive about the fact that we are on the wrong side of the cross. We talk about love, love, love, but it ought to be repent, repent, repent. John the Baptist came, and his message was *"Repent"* (Matt. 3:2). Jesus came with the same message: *"Repent"* (4:17). The Holy Spirit came, and the message was the same: repent, repent, repent and believe. (See Acts

2:38.) What has all this to do with Pentecost? Everything! It is the secret of our failure.

Daniel carried on his heart the burden of the people. He mourned for the captivity of Zion, he confessed his sin and the people's sin, and he identified himself with Israel until God made him a flame of fire. (See Daniel 9.) The result: a remnant returned to Zion to walk in the despised way of obedience to God.

Nehemiah was brokenhearted when he learned of the desolations of Jerusalem. He pleaded for months before God, confessing his sin and the sin of his people (see Nehemiah 1), and God opened the way, and the walls and gates were built up.

It is the spirit of deep repentance that is needed. You had an offering for foreign missionary work here yesterday. Fifty pounds was pledged, and you all seemed satisfied. May the Lord bless you for your gifts. They mean something, but they do not signify Pentecost. We have a lack of compassion. God says, *"You will seek Me and find Me, when you search for Me with all your heart"* (Jer. 29:13). Then the dry bones will move (see Ezekiel 37:5–10), and the Spirit will be poured out upon us without measure (John 3:34).

> *"Bring all the tithes into the storehouse, that there may be food in My house, and try Me now in this," says the LORD of hosts, "if I will not open for you the windows of heaven and pour out for you such blessing that there will not be room enough to receive it."* (Mal. 3:10)

With the baptism of the Holy Spirit comes a demolishing of the whole man and a compassion for the world.

Unconditional Surrender

Much that I see in the children of God these days is strange to me. Where does the fault lie for the state of things we see today? It is in the lack of a deep spirit of repentance. Weeping is not repentance; sorrow is not repentance. Repentance is turning away from sin and doing the work of righteousness and holiness. The baptism of the Holy Spirit brings a deep repentance and a demolished and impoverished spirit.

What can we do to receive it? Don't ask anymore! Instead, repent, repent, repent. God will hear and God will baptize. Will you repent? Is it possible, after we have been baptized with the Holy Spirit, to be satisfied with what we see? What made Jesus weep over Jerusalem? He had a heart of compassion. There are sin-sick souls everywhere. We need a baptism of love that goes to the bottom of the disease. We need to cry to God until He brings us up to the *"measure of the stature of the fullness of Christ"* (Eph. 4:13).

Jesus told a parable about *"a certain man [who] went down from Jerusalem to Jericho, and fell among thieves"* (Luke 10:30). Who among those who passed by and saw his predicament was his neighbor? The one who had mercy on him and helped him (vv. 36–37). Are you awake to the great fact that God has given you eternal life? With the power God has put at your disposal, how can you rest as you look out upon your neighbors? How we have sinned against God! How we lack this spirit of compassion! Do we weep as we look out upon the unsaved? If not, we are not Pentecost-full. Jesus was moved with compassion. Are you?

We have not yet grasped the plight of the heathen. Since my only daughter went to Africa, I have a little less dim idea of what it meant that God so loved the world that He gave Jesus (John 3:16). God gave Jesus. What does that mean? Compassion. *"You shall receive power when the Holy Spirit has come upon you"* (Acts 1:8). If you have no power, you have not repented. You say, "That's hard language." It is truth.

Who is your brother's keeper? (See Genesis 4:9.) Who is the son and heir? (See Galatians 4:7.) Are you salted? (See Matthew 5:13.) Do you have a pure life? Don't be fooled; don't live in a false position. The world wants to know how to be saved, and power is at our disposal. Will we meet the conditions? God says, "If you will, I will." God will do it.

Daniel knew the time in which he was living; he responded to God, and a nation was saved. Nehemiah met God's conditions for his time, and the city was rebuilt. God has made the conditions. He will pour out His Spirit.

If we do not go on, we will have it to face. It may be up to us to bring the Gospel to the nations. We can win the world for Jesus. We can turn the tap on. What is the condition? It is unconditional surrender. *"'Not by might nor by power, but by My Spirit,' says the LORD of hosts"* (Zech. 4:6). Depart from sin; holiness opens the windows of heaven. The Spirit of God will be poured out without measure, until the people say, *"What must* [we] *do to be saved?"* (Acts 16:30).

18

New Wine

t is a settled thing in the glory that in the fullness of time the latter rain has to be greater than the former. (See Zechariah 10:1; James 5:7.) Some of our hearts have been greatly moved by the former rain, but it is the latter rain we are crying out for. What will it be like when the fullness comes and the heart of God is satisfied?

On the Day of Pentecost, *"they were all filled with the Holy Spirit and began to speak with other tongues, as the Spirit gave them utterance"* (Acts 2:4). What a lovely thought that the Holy Spirit had such sway that the words were all His! We are having to learn, whether we like it or not, that our end is God's beginning. Then it is all God; the Lord Jesus stands forth in the midst with such divine glory, and men are impelled, filled, led so perfectly. Nothing else will meet the need of the world.

We see that there was something beautiful about Peter and John when we read that people *"realized that they had been with Jesus"* (4:13). There was something so real, so after the order of the Master, about them.

Now when they saw the boldness of Peter and John, and perceived that they were uneducated and untrained men, they marveled. And they realized that they had been with Jesus. (v. 13)

May all in the temple glorify Jesus; it can be so.

The one thing that was more marked than anything else in the life of Jesus was the fact that the people glorified God in Him. And when God is glorified and gets the right-of-way and the wholehearted attention of His people, everyone is as He is, filled with God. Whatever it costs, it must be. Let it be so. Filled with God! The only thing that will help people is to speak the latest thing God has given us from the glory.

There is nothing outside salvation. We are filled, immersed, clothed upon with the Spirit. There must be nothing felt, seen, or spoken about except the mighty power of the Holy Spirit. We are new creatures in Christ Jesus, baptized into a new nature. *"He who believes in Me, as the Scripture has said, out of his heart will flow rivers of living water"* (John 7:38). The very life of the risen Christ is to be in everything we are and do, moving us to do His will.

There is something we have not yet touched in the spiritual realm, but praise God for the thirst to be in this meeting! Praise God, the thirst is of God, the desire is of God, the plan is of God, the purpose is of God. It is God's plan, God's thought, God's vessel, and God's servant. We are in the world to meet the need, but we are not of the world or of its spirit. (See John 17:15–16.)

We are *"partakers of the divine nature"* (2 Pet. 1:4) to manifest the life of Jesus to the world. This is God incarnate in humanity.

New Wine

On the Day of Pentecost, *"others mocking said, 'They are full of new wine'"* (Acts 2:13). That is what we want, you say? *"New wine"*—a new order, a new inspiration, a new manifestation. New, new, new, new wine. A power all new in itself, as if you were born, as you are, into a new day, a new creation. *"No man ever spoke like this Man!"* (John 7:46).

This new wine has a freshness about it! It has a beauty about it! It has a quality about it! It creates in others the desire for the same taste. At Pentecost, some saw, but three thousand felt, tasted, and enjoyed. Some looked on; others drank with a new faith never before seen—a new manifestation, a new realization all divine, a new thing. It came straight from heaven, from the throne of the glorified Lord. It is God's purpose to fill us with that wine, to make us ready to burst forth with new rivers, with fresh energy, with no tired feeling.

God manifested in the flesh. That is what we want, and it is what God wants, and it satisfies everybody. All the people said, "We have never seen anything like it." (See Acts 2:7–12.) The disciples rejoiced in its being new; others were *"cut to the heart, [crying out] to Peter and the rest of the apostles, 'Men and brethren, what shall we do?'"* (v. 37).

> *Then Peter said to them, "Repent, and let every one of you be baptized in the name of Jesus Christ for the remission of sins; and you shall receive the gift of the Holy Spirit. For the promise is to you and to your children, and to all who are afar off, as many as the Lord our God will call." And with many other words he testified and exhorted them, saying, "Be saved from this perverse generation."* (vv. 38–40)

What shall we do? Men and brethren, what shall we do? Believe! Stretch out! Press on! Let there be a new entering in, a new passion to have it. We must be beside ourselves; we must drink deeply of the new wine so that multitudes may be satisfied and find satisfaction too.

The new wine must have a new wineskin—that is the necessity of a new vessel. (See Matthew 9:17.) If anything of the old is left, not put to death, destroyed, there will be a tearing and a breaking. The new wine and the old vessel will not work in harmony. It must be new wine and a new wineskin. Then there will be nothing to discard when Jesus comes.

> *For the Lord Himself will descend from heaven with a shout, with the voice of an archangel, and with the trumpet of God. And the dead in Christ will rise first. Then we who are alive and remain shall be caught up together with them in the clouds to meet the Lord in the air. And thus we shall always be with the Lord.* (1 Thess. 4:16–17)

The Spirit is continually working within us to change us until the day when we will be like Him:

> [The Lord Jesus Christ] *will transform our lowly body that it may be conformed to His glorious body, according to the working by which He is able even to subdue all things to Himself.* (Phil. 3:21)

I desire that all of you be so filled with the Spirit, so hungry, so thirsty, that nothing will satisfy you but seeing Jesus. We are to get more thirsty every day, more dry every day, until the floods come and the Master passes by, ministering to us and through us the same life, the same inspiration, so that *"as He is, so are we in this world"* (1 John 4:17).

When Jesus became the sacrifice for man, He was in great distress, but it was accomplished. It meant strong crying and tears (see Hebrews 5:7); it meant the cross manward but the glory heavenward. Glory descending on a cross! Truly, *"great is the mystery of godliness"* (1 Tim. 3:16). He cried, *"It is finished!"* (John 19:30). Let the cry never be stopped until the heart of Jesus is satisfied, until His plan for humanity is reached in the sons of God being manifested (Rom. 8:19) and in the earth being *"filled with the knowledge of the glory of the LORD, as the waters cover the sea"* (Hab. 2:14). Amen. Amen. Amen.

19

Questions and Answers about the Baptism

Q: Is the Holy Spirit a personality?

A: Yes, He is. He is not an "it," not an influence, but He is a presence, a power, a person, the third person of the Trinity. That is the reason why the Lord said, *"When He, the Spirit of truth, has come, He will guide you into all truth"* (John 16:13).

Q: If you do not receive the baptism of the Holy Spirit, will you be lost?

A: Certainly not. You are not saved by the Holy Spirit. You are saved by the Word of God and the blood of Jesus.

Q: Is it as necessary to urge people to seek the baptism of the Holy Spirit as it is to urge them to be saved?

A: No, because the baptism of the Holy Spirit cannot come to anybody until he is saved. And a person could go to heaven without the baptism of the Holy Spirit—the thief on the cross did. You must understand that the most important thing today is getting people saved. But do not forget that after you are saved, you must seek so that you receive *"the Promise of the Father"* (Acts 1:4).

Q: The Holy Spirit said through John the Baptist, "[Jesus] *will baptize you with the Holy Spirit and fire"* (Matt. 3:11). Is it necessary that I receive the baptism of fire, and can I receive the Holy Spirit before I receive the baptism of fire?

A: It is one and the same thing. There is only one Holy Spirit, only one baptism, only one reception of the Spirit. When He comes in, He comes to abide.

We can't always give all the figurative descriptions of the Holy Spirit, but the fire of the Holy Spirit is more than figurative. It causes assimilation. The Holy Spirit causes our whole being to become assimilated to the divine nature. When He comes in, you will feel fire going through your body. You will feel a burning of all inward corruption.

The baptism of the Holy Spirit is essential for bringing into you a divine, holy fire that burns up all dross and quickens all purity, making you ablaze so that perfect love may continue.

The baptism of the Holy Spirit and the baptism of fire are one and the same. The baptism is the infilling of the divine third person of the Trinity.

Q: But on the Day of Pentecost, the fire fell upon them as tongues of fire, and afterward the Holy Spirit came. Will you explain that?

A: Before there were tongues of fire, there first was the *"rushing mighty wind"* (Acts 2:2). Let me explain the importance of this by looking at the life of our Lord. Jesus was a person, but He was a person of ideal perfection; the Father manifested all fullness in Him (Col. 2:9). And yet when all fullness came, it was necessary for Jesus to receive the flow of the Spirit's breath to formulate the Word; the Spirit breathed and Jesus said the words. Christ said, *"The words that I speak unto you I speak not of myself: but the Father that dwelleth in me, he doeth the works"* (John 14:10 KJV). The Spirit was the breath, the power, that was making the language.

Now, why did the Holy Spirit have to come at Pentecost? Simply because when Jesus was here, He was local. But the Holy Spirit can fill people in England, in America, in China, in Africa, in the islands of the sea, everywhere, all over the world. When He came, the breath, the power could fill the whole universe because it was the breath of the mighty power of God Himself.

Also, the Holy Spirit was a flame. Tongues of fire—what could be more inspiring? Flames of fire, tongues of fire burning up what was inflammable within. The disciples saw this on the Day of Pentecost, and it has been seen many times since then. But they were not baptized in the wind; they were not baptized in the fire. When were they baptized? When the wind and the fire got inside and caused eruption.

Q: Can a person receive the baptism of the Holy Spirit before being sanctified?

A: Yes. Do you know what it is to be saved? As you go on with God, you are being saved, and the more you go on with God, the more confident you are that you are saved. It was an accomplished fact that you were saved when you believed, but you are being saved as you walk in the light to a greater depth of knowledge of salvation. You were sanctified, but you are also being sanctified according to light, and you are not what you were yesterday.

Light, light, light! When you received the Holy Spirit, it is certain that the Lord was pleased with the place at which you had arrived, but it is not where you are going to. Every believer is sanctified, but no believer has received sanctification who does not also have an increased sanctification. There is no man being saved today who does not need to have an increased salvation, truth upon truth, *"line upon line"* (Isa. 28:10), knowing that he is ripe for heaven but that he is also going on to perfection. He is being changed *"from glory to glory"* (2 Cor. 3:18). The process is wonderful: being saved, being sanctified, being made ready every day!

Q: Is sanctification a definite work of grace?

A: Yes, and salvation also. And the next day, you will find out that as light comes, you will be like Isaiah in the presence of God; you will find you need another cleansing. (See Isaiah 6:5–7.) Light makes cleansing necessary.

Q: After being baptized in water, if one goes back in sin and then repents, is it necessary to be baptized again?

A: There has to come into your life a real knowledge that after you have had hands laid upon you, you do not have to expect that hands will need to be laid upon you again. After you have received the baptism, you are not to expect to be baptized again, in water or anywhere else. The Word of God is very clear; as you go on to perfection, you are leaving the first principles. You are leaving them behind because God says, "Come on!" Don't repeat anything that has passed by. Believe it is finished.

Q: Are the results mentioned in Mark 16:17–18 meant only for those who are baptized with the Holy Spirit?

A: Thousands of people who have never received the baptism of the Holy Spirit are very specially led and blessed in healing the sick. Some of the finest people that I ever knew have never come into the same experience as I am in today regarding the baptism of the Holy Spirit, yet they are mightily and wonderfully used in healing all kinds of sicknesses. But they do not have what is in the sixteenth chapter of Mark.

Only baptized believers speak in tongues. The Scripture says, "If you believe, you will lay

217

hands on the sick" and "If you believe, you will speak in new tongues." (See Mark 16:17–18.) This means that after the Holy Spirit comes, you are in the place of command. You can command. How do I know this? Because Paul, in 2 Timothy 1, was very clear when he said, *"Stir up the gift"* (v. 6). What was the trouble with Timothy? He was downcast. He was a young man who had been called out by Paul, but he had been among other clergymen. Because of his youth, he had been somewhat put off to the side, and he was grieved. Paul found him in a distressed place, so Paul stirred him up.

Every one of you, if you have faith, can *"stir up the gift"* within you. The Holy Spirit can be so manifested in you that you can speak in utterances with tongues as He gives you the ability, even though you may not have actually received the gift of tongues. And I believe that everybody baptized in the Holy Spirit has a right to allow the Spirit to have perfect control and to speak every day, morning, noon, and night, in this way.

Therefore, do not put out your hand to stop anybody who is doing good, but encourage him to do good; then bring him into the baptism of much good.

Q: When the Lord gives an interpretation of tongues, does He give it to the interpreter while the tongues are being given or when the interpretation is given?

Questions and Answers about the Baptism

A: The interpretation is not known to the interpreter at the time the tongues are given. The interpreter speaks as the Spirit gives him unction; he does not know what he is going to say or what he is saying. He speaks as the Spirit gives him liberty. Interpretation is like tongues. You do not know what you are saying when you speak in tongues. Likewise, you don't know what you are saying when you give interpretation. But you know what you have said.

Q: I have been waiting for the baptism of the Holy Spirit for a long time. I have been told that if I will say "Glory!" or "Hallelujah!" until I have lost myself, I will receive, but so far I have not received.

A: You have had a great deal of things in your mind as to what ought to bring the baptism, and you are forgetting what will bring it, and that is Jesus. Jesus is the Baptizer. As soon as you are ready, He will fill you.

Q: Can anyone receive the baptism of the Holy Spirit in his own room?

A: Yes. I believe that after hands have been laid upon you to receive the Holy Spirit, you can go away believing that you will certainly receive, whether it is in your bed or anywhere else. I laid my hands on a very remarkable man in London; we considered him one of the finest men we had. He went home and received the baptism of the Holy Spirit in his bed.

Remember that no person is a baptizer. Jesus is the only Baptizer, and you never get away from His presence. He is with you in your bedroom; He is with you at your workplace; He is with you everywhere. *"Lo, I am with you always"* (Matt. 28:20).